The Nature and Method of Secret Prayer

by Samuel Lee
with chapters by C. Matthew McMahon

Copyright Information

The Nature and Method of Secret Prayer by Samuel Lee, with chapters by C. Matthew McMahon
Edited by Therese B. McMahon

Copyright ©2019 by Puritan Publications and A Puritan's Mind®

Some language and grammar has been updated from any original manuscripts. Any change in wording or punctuation has not changed the intent or meaning of the original author(s) and has been made to aid the modern reader.

Published by Puritan Publications
A Ministry of A Puritan's Mind® in Crossville, TN.
Visit our ring of Reformed Sites:
www.apuritansmind.com
www.puritanpublications.com
https://reformed.org
https://crta.org
www.gracechapeltn.com

All rights reserved. No part of this publication may be reproduced, stored in a retrieval system or transmitted in any form by any means, electronic, mechanical, photocopy, recording or otherwise, without the prior permission of the publisher, except as provided by USA copyright law.

This Print Edition, 2019
Electronic Edition, 2019

Manufactured in the United States of America

ISBN: 978-1-62663-335-3
eISBN: 978-1-62663-334-6

Table of Contents

Meet Samuel Lee 4

Practical Praying 10

Chapter 1: The Nature of Prayer 21

Chapter 2: The Depth of the Text 24

Chapter 3: The Duty of Secret Prayer 28

Chapter 4: Managing Secret Prayer 32

Chapter 5: Directions for Secret Prayer 48

Chapter 6: Answered Prayer 62

Chapter 7: Further Questions 72

Chapter 8: Ejaculatory Prayer 77

Chapter 9: Uses 81

Other Helpful Books by Puritan Publications 88

Meet Samuel Lee
Edited by C, Matthew McMahon

Samuel Lee (1625–1691) was a puritan divine, born in 1625. He was the only son of Samuel Lee, haberdasher of small wares in Fish Street Hill, London. He was probably connected with the Lees of Cheshire, for which county he had "an exuberant and natural love."[1] He was educated at St. Paul's School under Dr. Gill, entered Magdalen Hall, Oxford, in 1647, and was created M.A. by the parliamentary visitors on April 14, 1648. He was elected fellow of Wadham College on October 3, 1648, was recommended for a fellowship at Merton in 1649, and was appointed to one at All Souls in 1650, but nevertheless remained at Wadham. He was elected as the proctor in 1651, objecting on the ground of insufficient standing being overruled by the parliamentary visitors, and he was admitted April 9of that year. He was bursar of his college in 1648, 1650, and 1664, sub-warden in 1652, and dean in 1653. From about 1650 he was a constant preacher in and near Oxford, although he had not received orders from a bishop. After preaching in London he was, in 1654, recalled to his duties at Wadham by the visitors of that year. He gave up his position on June 13, 1656, and vacated his fellowship in 1657.

---

[1] See *Chron. Cestrense*, p. 1.

In July 1655 he was made minister of St. Botolph's, Bishopsgate, by Cromwell, and occupied the church until August 1659, when he was removed by a committee of the Hump parliament. Towards the end of the Protectorate he was also lecturer of St. Helen's, Bishopsgate. After the Restoration he became a member of Dr. John Owen's congregation in Leadenhall Street, preached in various London churches, and occasionally resided on an estate he possessed at Bignal, near Bicester in Oxfordshire. On the death of John Rowe (October 12, 1677) he became joint pastor with Theophilus Gale of Howe's congregation in Baker's Court, Holborn; but in the following year, on Gale's death, removed to Newington Green, where he was minister of an independent congregation until 1686.

Lee migrated to New England in 1686, and on the formation of a church at Bristol in Rhode Island was chosen minister on May 8, 1687, but after the revolution he decided to return to England. He sailed from Boston October 2, 1691. His ship was seized by a French privateer and taken to St. Malo. His wife and daughter were separated from him and, unknown to him, were sent to England. Overcome with grief, he died at St. Malo of a fever about December 1691, and was buried obscurely outside the town. In his will he left property to his wife Martha, and books and manuscripts to his four daughters, Rebecca, Anna, Lydia, and Elizabeth. His daughter Lydia married John George, a merchant of Boston, and after George's death became, on July 5, 1716, the third wife of Cotton Mather. She died in January 1733-1734.

Lee was a good scholar, speaking Latin fluently, and being well acquainted with chemistry and medicine. Cotton Mather considered that "hardly ever a more universally learned person trod the American strand."[2] He had studied astrology, but afterwards destroyed many books and manuscripts on the subject that he had collected. Lee inclined more to Independency than to Presbyterianism, but rigidly professed neither. Bishop Wilkins, his former tutor, vainly urged him to conform at the Restoration. He was charitable, and contributed generously to the Hungarian ministers taking refuge in England.

His works:

Lee wrote, in the name of the printer, H. Hall, a Latin epistle to the reader, for the fifth edition of Helvicus' "Theatrum Historicum," Oxford, 1651, and continued the work from 1629 to the date of publication.[3] The epistle was reprinted in the sixth edition, Oxford, 1662, when Lee further supplied a treatise, "De Antiquitate Academiæ Oxoniensis," *etc.*, and "Tractatulus ad Periodum Julianum spectans" (both in the name of the printer), and continued the work to

---

[2] *Magnalia*, edit. 1853, i. 602
[3] See pages 166-185 of that volume.

1662. His "Chronicum Cestrenæ" was published in Daniel King's "Vale Royal of England," London, 1656.[4]

Other of his works were:
1. 'Orbis Miraculum, or the Temple of Solomon,' London, 1659, 1665, printed at the expense of the university of Oxford. This book was plagiarized by one Christopher Kelly, who reproduced the last part as 'Solomon's Temple spiritualized' at Dublin in 1803. It was again published as Kelly's in 1820, at Philadelphia.[5]
2. 'De Excidio Anti-christi,' 1659.
3. 'What means may be used towards the Conversion of our Carnal Relations?' London, 1661; in Annesley's 'Morning Exercises,' 1677 and 1844.
4. 'Contemplations on Mortality,' London, 1669.
5. 'The Visibility of the True Church,' in Vincent's 'Morning Exercises,' 1675; Annesley, 1845.
6. 'How to manage Secret Prayer,' in Annesley's 'Supplement,' 1676 and 1844.
7. 'The Triumph of Mercy,' London, 1677; Boston, 1718.
8. 'Ecclesia Gemens' (anon.), London, 1677, 1678, 1679.
9. 'Israel Redux,' London, 1677, 1678, 1679, including a hitherto unprinted essay on the Ten Tribes by Giles Fletcher, LL.D.
10. 'The Joy of Faith,' Boston, 1687; London, 1689. 'A Discourse of the Nature, Property, and Fruit of the

---

[4] See pages 3-25 of that volume.
[5] Notes and Queries, 3rd ser. xi. 375, 486.

Christian Faith,' London, 1702, mentioned by Wood, appears to be a fresh issue of the same work.

After Lee's death appeared "The Great Day of Judgment," an assize sermon, from Boston, 1692, 1694, and 1696. He published a collection of thirty sermons by John Rowe, under the title of "Emmanuel, or the Love of Christ," London, 1680, and is believed to have been the "S.L." who wrote the preface to Thomas Mall's "History of the Martyrs epitomised." "An Answer to many Queries relative to America," mentioned among his works under the date of 1690, was probably never printed. A manuscript letter of 1690, bearing a similar title, from Lee to "the very learned Dr. Nehemiah Grew," is among the Sloane collection of letters in the British Museum (Add. MS. 4051).

For further reading:
Allen's *American Biog. Dict.*; Wood's *Athenæ* (Bliss) ii. cols. 345-7; Wood's *Fasti* (Bliss) ii. cols. 111, 164; Palmer's *Nonconformist's Memorial*, i. 104-6; Calamy's *Contin.* pp. 54-5; Gardiner's *Admission Registers of St. Paul's School*, p. 463; Gardiner's *Registers of Wadham College*, pp. 172-3; *Registers of Visitors of Oxford* (Camden Society), pp. 476, 525-6, 562; Wood's *Hist. and Antiq.* (Gutch), App. p. 137; *Cal State Papers*, Dom. Ser. 1655, p. 254; Churchwardens' *Yearly Accounts of St. Botolph's*, 1655-9 (manuscript); Commons' *Journals*, vii. 770; Thomson's *Life of Owen*, p. 139; Wilson's *Dissenting Churches*, iii. 168; Wilson's MSS. in Dr.

Williams's library (London and Suburbs), p. 256; Drake's *Cotton Mather*, p. 14; Sprague's *American Pulpit*, pp. 209-10; Dunn's *Eminent Divines*, pp. 28-9; Kennett's *Reg.* p. 673; Halkett and Laing's *Dict. of Anon, and Pseudon.* Lit.; Brit. Mus. Cat.

Practical Praying
by C. Matthew McMahon

As much as prayer seems to be simple, it is also very biblically complicated. It is the Christian's security about which he should be "always praying," (1 Thess. 5:17). But how does he do this, and what is the method and nature of this prayer he is to pray "always?" Prayer is the Word of God formed into an argument and retorted back to God again. It relies heavily on knowledge of the Word. Practically speaking, prayer is the *soul* breathing itself into the heart of its heavenly Father. It is a duty performed to God by sensible and believing souls, in which they ask for things according to his will, in the name of Christ, by the power of the Spirit, with thanksgiving for what already has been received. Ephesians 6:18, "Praying always with all prayer and supplication in the Spirit, and watching thereunto with all perseverance and supplication for all saints."

The following outline is a simplified flow chart of the *Lord's Prayer*, with some notes to aid the praying Christian in that ordinance and duty before God. It is taken from the *1647 Westminster Larger Catechism*, and has been expanded.

Lord, I am your servant, take all the faculties of my soul, and the members of my body, improve it all, lay out everything to your own praise to the uttermost, to bring glory to your great Name, (1 John 5:14; Matt. 6:2-13; Luke 11:2-4).

After this manner pray ye, (Matt. 6:9).
> The model and pattern of all our prayers.

Our Father, which art in heaven, (Matt. 6:9).
> In what sense is God a Father?
>> By creation, (Mal. 2:10)
>> By election, (Eph. 1:4)
>> By grace, (1 John 3:9)
>
> In what sense is God in heaven?
>> By His manifested glory.
>> Where the angels worship Him.
>> Where the departed saints worship him.
>> Where he is high and lofty and lifted up (Isa. 6)
>
> We are to pray for:

The Whole Church of Christ Upon the Earth, (Eph. 6:18; Psa. 28:9)
> Magistrates, (1 Tim. 2:1-2)
> Minister, (Col. 4:3)
> Ourselves, (Gen. 32:11)
> Our Brethren, (James 5:16)
> Our Enemies, (Matt. 5:44)
> All Kinds of Men, (1 Tim. 2:1-2)

Hallowed be thy name, (Matt 6:9; 1 Peter 1:15-16)
> That God would by his grace enable and incline us and others to know, to acknowledge, and

highly to esteem him. Adoration of his titles,[4] attributes,[5] ordinances, word,[6] works, and whatsoever he is pleased to make himself known by;[7] and to glorify him in thought, word,[8] and deed:[9] that he would prevent and remove atheism,[10] ignorance,[11] idolatry,[12] profaneness,[13] and: whatsoever is dishonorable to him;[14] and, by his overruling providence, direct and dispose of all things to his own glory.[15] ([4.] Psa. 83:18; [5.] Psa. 86:10-13, 15; [6.] 2 Thess. 3:1; Psa. 138:1-3; 147:19-20; 2 Cor. 2:14-15; [7.] Psa. ch. 8; ch. 145; [8.] Psa. 19:14; 103:1; [9.] Phil. 1:9, 11; [10.] Psa. 67:1-4; [11.] Eph. 1:17-18; [12.] Psa. 97:7; [13.] Psa. 74:18, 22-23; [14.] 2 Kings 19:15-16; [15.] 2 Chr. 20:6, 10-12; Psa. ch. 83; 140:4, 8).

    Personal Holiness
        A good steward over holiness
        1 Peter 1:15-16. Holiness and the reflection of your holiness.
        High Thoughts of God's Holiness
            Cultivating the desire to be more holy.
        Have a Constraint in Holiness
        Being Constant in Holiness.
Having High Thoughts of God
    Considering His Attributes
        Such as Triune, Holy, Simple, Faithful, Independent,

Immutable, Infinite, Immense, Eternal, all-knowing, Everywhere Present, Spirit, being *captivated* by His attributes, by the Incarnation, by the Atonement.

Thy kingdom come, (Matt 6:10)
    The Expansion of the Kingdom
        What is my Role in the Expansion of the Kingdom?

Inward (Col. 3:1-4) and Outward (Acts 13:47)
    Inward in the Mind
    Outward in Ministry
        Acknowledging ourselves and all mankind to be by nature under the dominion of sin and Satan, (Eph. 2:2-3).
        We pray that the kingdom of sin and Satan may be destroyed, (Psa. 68:1, 18; Rev. 12:10-11).

We pray for the gospel propagated throughout the world,[4] the Jews called,[5] the fulness of the Gentiles brought in;[6] the church furnished with all gospel officers and ordinances,[7] purged from corruption,[8] countenanced and maintained by the civil magistrate:[9] that the ordinances of Christ may be purely dispensed, and made effectual to the converting of those that are yet in their sins, and the confirming, comforting, and building up of those that are already converted:[10] that Christ would rule in our hearts here,[11] and hasten the time of his second coming, and our reigning with him forever:[12] and that he would be pleased so to exercise the kingdom of his power in all the world, as may best conduce to these ends.[13] ([4.] 2 Thess. 3:1; [5.] Rom. 10:1; [6.] John 17:9, 20; Rom. 11:25-26; Psa. 67; [7.] Matt. 9:38; 2 Thess. 3:1; [8.] Mal. 1:11; Zeph. 3:9; [9.] 1 Tim. 2:1-2; [10.] Acts 4:29-30; Eph. 6:18-20; Rom. 15:29-30, 32; 2 Thess. 1:11; 2:16-17; [11.] Eph. 3:14-20; [12.] Rev. 22:20; [13.] Isa. 64:1-2; Rev. 4:8-11)

Thy will be done in earth, as it is in heaven, (Matt 6: 10).

The Will of God, (Ezekiel 10:13, God Commands the Wheels in His Providence) Acknowledging, that by nature we and all men are not only utterly unable and unwilling to know and do the will of God,[2] but prone to rebel against his word,[3] to repine and murmur against his providence,[4] and wholly inclined to do the will of the flesh, and of the devil:[5] we pray, that God would by his Spirit take away from ourselves and others all blindness,[6] weakness,[7] indisposedness,[8] and perverseness of heart;[9] and by his grace make us able and willing to know, do, and submit to his will in all things,[10] with the like humility,[11] cheerfulness,[12] faithfulness,[13] diligence,[14] zeal,[15] sincerity,[16] and constancy,[17] as the angels do in heaven.[18] ([2.] Rom. 7:18; Job 21:14; 1 Cor. 2:14; [3.] Rom. 8:7; [4.] Exod. 17:7; Num. 14:2; [5.] Eph. 2:2; [6.] Eph. 1:17-18; [7.] Eph. 3:16; [8.] Matt. 26:40-41; [9.] Jer. 31:18-19; [10.] Psa. 119:1, 8, 35-36; Acts 21:14; [11.] Micah 6:8; [12.] Psa. 100:2; Job 1:21; 2 Sam. 15:25-26; [13.] Isa. 38:3; [14.] Psa. 119:4-5; [15.] Rom. 12:11; [16.] Psa. 119:80; [17.] Psa. 119:112; [18.] Isa. 6:2-3; Psa. 103:20-21; Matt. 18:10).

Yielding to His Providence, (Ezekiel 10:13).
What is God's will in the future?
> Redeeming the Time
> God's Will in All Things, (Psalm 119:60)
>> What is God's will in my life?
>> Health, jobs, family matters, etc.
>> Personal Requests

Give us this day our daily bread, (Matt 6:11)
> Provisions of all Kinds

Acknowledging, that in Adam, and by our own sin, we have forfeited our right to all the outward blessings of this life, and deserve to be wholly deprived of them by God, and to have them cursed to us in the use of them;[2] and that neither they of themselves are able to sustain us,[3] nor we to merit,[4] or by our own industry to procure them;[5] but prone to desire,[6] get,[7] and use them unlawfully:[8] we pray for ourselves and others, that both they and we, waiting upon the providence of God from day to day in the use of lawful means, may, of his free gift, and as to his fatherly wisdom shall seem best, enjoy a competent portion of them;[9] and have the same continued and blessed unto us in our holy and comfortable use of them,[10] and contentment in them;[11] and be kept from all things that are contrary to our temporal support and comfort.[12] ([2.] Gen. 2:17, 3:17; Rom. 8:20-22; Jer. 5:25; Deut. 28:15-68; [3.] Deut. 8:3; [4.] Gen. 32:10; [5.] Deut. 8:17-18; [6.] Jer. 6:13; Mark 7:21-22; [7.] Hosea 12:7; [8.] James 4:3; [9.] Gen. 28:20; 43:12-14; Eph. 4:28; 2 Thess. 3:11-12; Phil. 4:6; [10.] 1 Tim. 4:3-5; [11.] 1 Tim. 6:6-8; 12. Prov. 30:8-9).

Daily Bread, (Proverbs 30:8-9)

Forgive us our debts, as we forgive our debtors, (Matt. 6:12)

Forgiveness, (Psalm 119:94)
Reminded of Justification and Christ's Imputation (Titus 3:7)

> Acknowledging, that we and all others are guilty both of original and actual sin, and thereby become debtors to the justice of God; and that neither we, nor any other creature, can make the least satisfaction for that debt:[2] we pray for ourselves and others, that God of his free grace would, through the obedience and satisfaction of Christ, apprehended and applied by faith, acquit us both from the guilt and punishment of sin,[3] accept us in his Beloved;[4] continue his favor and grace to us,[5] pardon our daily failings,[6] and fill us with peace and joy, in giving us daily more and more assurance of forgiveness;[7] which we are the rather emboldened to ask, and encouraged to expect, when we have this testimony in ourselves, that we from the heart forgive others their offenses.[8] ([2.] Rom. 3:9-22; Matt. 18:24-25; Psa. 130:3-4; [3.] Rom. 3:24-26; Heb. 9:22; [4.] Eph. 1:6-7; [5.] 2 Peter 1:2; [6.] Hosea 14:2; Jer. 14:7; [7.] Rom. 15:13; Psa. 51:7-10, 12; [8.] Luke 11:4; Matt. 6:14-15; 18:35).

Practical Praying

And lead us not into temptation, but deliver us from evil (or *deliver us from the evil one*), (Matt. 6:13).

> Acknowledging, that the most wise, righteous, and gracious God, for divers holy and just ends, may so order things, that we may be assaulted, foiled, and for a time led captive by temptations;[2] that Satan,[3] the world,[4] and the flesh, are ready powerfully to draw us aside, and ensnare us;[5] and that we, even after the pardon of our sins, by reason of our corruption,[6] weakness, and want of watchfulness,[7] are not only subject to be tempted, and forward to expose ourselves unto temptations,[8] but also of ourselves unable and unwilling to resist them, to recover out of them, and to improve them;[9] and worthy to be left under the power of them:[10] we pray, that God would so overrule the world and all in it,[11] subdue the flesh,[12] and restrain Satan,[13] order all things,[14] bestow and bless all means of grace,[15] and quicken us to watchfulness in the use of them, that we and all his people may by his providence be kept from being tempted to sin;[16] or, if tempted, that by his Spirit we may be powerfully supported and enabled to stand in the hour of temptation;[17] or when fallen, raised again and recovered out of it,[18] and have a sanctified use and improvement thereof:[19] that our sanctification and salvation

may be perfected,[20] Satan trodden under our feet,[21] and we fully freed from sin, temptation, and all evil, forever.[22] ([2.] 2 Chr. 32:31; [3.] 1 Chr. 21:1; [4.] Luke 21:34; Mark 4:19; [5.] James 1:14; [6.] Gal. 5:17; [7.] Matt. 26:41; [8.] Matt. 26:69-72; Gal. 2:11-14; 2 Chr. 18:3; 19:2; [9.] Rom. 7:23-24; 1 Chr. 21:1-4; 2 Chr. 16:7-10; [10.] Psa. 81:11-12; [11.] John 17:15; [12.] Psa. 51:10; 119:133; [13.] 2 Cor. 12:7-8; [14.] 1 Cor. 10:12-13; [15.] Heb. 13:20-21; [16.] Matt. 26:41; Psa. 19:13; [17.] Eph. 3:14-17; 1 Thess. 3:13; Jude 1:24; [18.] Psa. 51:12; [19.] 1 Peter 5:8-10; [20.] 2 Cor. 13:7, 9; [21.] Rom. 16:20; Zech. 3:2; Luke 22:31-32; [22.] John 17:15; 1 Thess. 5:23).

    Temptation, (James 1:12)
    Spiritual Combat, (Gal. 5:17)
      A Continued Daily Strategy

For thine is the kingdom, and the power, and the glory, forever. Amen. (Matt. 6:13)

This teaches us to enforce our petitions with arguments,[2] which are to be taken, not from any worthiness in ourselves, or in any other creature, but from God;[3] and with our prayers to join praises,[4] ascribing to God alone eternal sovereignty, omnipotency, and glorious excellency;[5] in regard whereof, as he is able and willing to help us,[6] so we by faith are emboldened to plead with him that he would,[7] and quietly to rely upon him, that he will fulfill our requests.[8] And, to testify this our desire and assurance, we say, Amen.[9] ([2.]Rom. 15:30; [3.] Dan. 9:4, 7-9, 16-19; [4.] Phil. 4:6; [5.] 1 Chr. 29:10-13; [6.] Eph. 3:20-21; Luke 11:13; [7.] 2 Chr. 20:6, 11; [8.] 2 Chr. 14:11; [9.] 1 Cor. 14:16; Rev. 22:20-21)

Conclude with Petitions for Others

Chapter 1:
The Nature of Prayer

"But thou, when thou prayest, enter into thy closet, and when thou hast shut thy door, pray to thy Father which is in secret; and thy Father which seeth in secret shall reward thee openly," (Matt. 6:6).

We have here our blessed Lord's instruction for the management of secret prayer, the crown and glory of a child of God: in which observe the following.

1. The direction prescribed for our manner in secret duty, is set in three things:

(1.) Enter into thy closet. The word ταμιειον Hesychius interprets by αποκρυφον οικημα, "a secret or recluse habitation;" and Suidas, by θησαυρος, "a hiding-place for treasures," by a metonymy.[1] The LXX, (such as we have it), uses the Hebrew word חָדָר so frequently by ταμειον, that we do not need to inquire any further; as Gen. 43:30; Exod. 8:3; 2 Sam. 13:10; 1 Kings 1:15; and otherwise, for "a chamber, a parlor, a bed-chamber." Sometimes, the word חוֹר, is used of "a hole, cleft, or cavern in a rock," as Isaiah 42:22, which they render also by τρωγλη and οπη. The etymology of the word, being

---

[1] *Metonymy* is the substitution of the name of an attribute or adjunct for that of the thing meant, for example calling someone a *suit* for a *business executive*.

derived απο του τεμνειν, from holes, pits, caves "cut out" in rocks, shows that it notes secret places for retirements or repositories. It is accordingly rendered by "secret chambers," in Matt. 24:26, and by "closets" in Luke 12:3.

(2.) Shut the door. Or, "lock it," as the word insinuates, Κλεισας την θυραν, (from where κλεις, "a key," is deduced; and they are both put together, as appears by Rev. 3:7; 20:1, 3), implying that we must "bar or bolt" it.

(3.) Pray to thy Father in secret. "Father," which is *pietatis et potestatis appellatio*, as Tertullian notes, "a name hinting both piety and power." To *thy Father*, noting both propriety and intimacy.

2. A gracious promise. This may be branched into three parts:

(1). For thy Father sees thee in secret. His eye is on you with a gracious aspect when you are withdrawn from all the world.

(2.) He will reward thee. Αποδωσει, or, as Ambrose reads it, *reddet*. So the word is sometimes translated by "rendering," (Matt. 22:21; Rom. 2:6; 13:7), by "delivering," (Matt. 27:58; Luke 9:42), by "yielding" or "affording," (Heb. 12:11; Rev. 22:2). All of this comes to this, "He will return your prayers or your requests amply and abundantly into your heart."

(3.) He will do it openly. Εν τω φανερω, "perspicuously and manifestly" before the world sometimes, and most plentifully and, exuberantly before men and angels at the great day. Secret prayers shall have open and public answers.

3. Here is a demonstration of sincerity, from the right performance of this duty, set forth by the antithesis, "But thou shalt not be as the hypocrites." (Matt. 6:5).

When. That is, as often as you pray *by yourself. Enter.* Not only your house, your hall, or your common chamber, but your closet. The most secret and retired privacy. *Shut the door.* That others may neither discern you, nor rush in suddenly on you. *He shall reward thee.* That is, he shall answer you and perform your request as a gracious return to your secret sincerity. God is pleased by promise to make himself a debtor to secret prayer. It brings nothing to God but empty hands and naked hearts; to show that reward, in Scripture, does not flow in on the streams of merit, but all of grace. It is "monkish divinity" to assert otherwise, for, what merit, strictly taken, can there be in prayer? The mere asking of mercy cannot merit it at the hands of God, who, out of our most sincere petitions (being at best impregnated with sinful mixtures) might take-up matter enough to fling as the dung of our sacrifices in our faces, (Mal. 2:3). We halt like Jacob both in and after our choicest and strongest wrestlings; but such is the grace of our heavenly Father, who spies that little sincerity of our hearts in secret, that he is pleased to accept us in his Beloved, and to smell a savor of rest in the fragrant perfumes and odors of his intercession.

Chapter 2:
The Depth of the Text

Here I would like to draw forth several notes, yet I shall treat only one, containing the marrow and nerves of the text.

OBSERVATION. That secret prayer, duly managed, is the mark of a sincere heart, and has the promise of a gracious return. Prayer is the soul's discussion with God; and secret prayer is a conference with God, on admission into the privy-chamber of heaven. When you have shut your own closet, when God and your soul are alone, with this key you open the chambers of Paradise, and enter the closet of divine love. When you are confined as in a curious labyrinth from the tumultuous world, and entered into that garden of Lebanon in the midst of your closet, your soul, like a spiritual Dædalus, takes to itself the wings of faith and prayer, and flies into the midst of heaven among the cherubim. I may describe secret prayer "the invisible flight of the soul into the bosom of God." Out of this heavenly closet rises Jacob's ladder, whose rounds are all of light. Its foot stands upon the basis of the covenant in your heart, its top reaches the throne of grace. When your reins have instructed you in the night-season with holy petitions, when your soul has desired him in the night, then with your spirit within you, will you seek him early, (Psalm 16:7; Isa. 26:9). When the door of your heart is shut, and the windows of your eyes sealed-up from all vain and worldly objects, up you mount, and have a place given to you to walk among angels "that stand by" the throne of God, (Zech. 3:7). In secret prayer the soul, like Moses, is in the backside of the desert, and talks with the angel of the covenant in the fiery bush, (Exod. 3:1–6). Here is Isaac in the field at evening, meditating and praying to the God of his father Abraham, (Gen. 24:63). Here is Elijah under the juniper-tree at Rithmah in the wilderness, and later in the cave hearkening to the still small voice of God, (1 Kings 19:4, 12). Here is Christ and the spouse alone in the wine-cellar, and the banner of love over her, (Song of Songs 2:4); where she utters *verba dimidiata, ubi bibit ebriam sobrietatem Spiritûs*, "And be not drunk with wine, wherein is excess; but be filled with the Spirit," (Eph. 5:18). Here we find Nathanael under the fig-tree, though it may be at secret prayer, yet under a beam of the eye of Christ, (John 1:48). There sits Augustine in the garden alone, sighing with the Psalmist, *Usque quò, Domine?* "How long, O Lord?" and listening to the voice of God, *Tolle lege,* "Take up the Bible and read."

It is true, hypocrites may pray, and pray alone, and pray long, and receive their reward, ὧαρ' ὧν επιθυμουσιν αυτοι, "from such whose observation they desire;" but they take no true delight in secret devotion, they have no spring of affection to God, (Matt. 23:14). But, "O my dove," Christ says, "that art in the clefts of the rock, let me hear thy voice; for the melody thereof is sweet." (Song of Songs 2:14). A weeping countenance and a wounded spirit are most beautiful prospects to the eye of heaven. When a broken heart pours-out repentant tears, like streams from the rock smitten by the rod of Moses's law in the hand of a Mediator; O, how amiable in the sight of God! "Out of the depths have I cried unto thee," (Psalm 130:1). As Chrysostom describes this, Κατωθεν απο της καρδιας σου ἑλκυσον την φωνην· μυστηριον ὦοιησον σου την ευχην. "Draw sighs from the furrows of thy heart, *e sulco pectoris:* let thy prayer become a hidden mystery of divine secrets." Do this like good Hezekiah upon the bed with his face to the wall, that none might observe him, (Isa. 38:2, 5); or like our blessed Lord, that grand Example, who retired into solitudes and mountains apart from everyone, and saw by night the illustrious face of his heavenly Father in prayer. The reasons for this follow.

1. Because a sincere heart busies itself about heart-work to mortify sin, to quicken grace, to observe and resist temptations, to secure and advance his evidences; and therefore, the heart is so much conversant in secret prayer. The glory of the king's daughter shines within, arrayed with clothes of gold, (Psalm 45:13); but they are the spangled and glittering hangings of the closet of her heart, when she entertains communion with her Lord. The more a saint converses with his own heart, the more he searches his spiritual wants, and feels his spiritual joys.

2. Because a sincere heart aims at the eye of God. He knows that God, being a Spirit, loves to converse

with our spirits, and "to speak to the heart" more than the outward ear, (Hosea 2:14). He labors to walk before God, as being always in his sight, but especially when he presents himself at the footstool of mercy. Because God is invisible, την ευχην σου τοιαυτην ειναι βουλεται, an invisible God is delighted with invisible prayers, when no eye sees but his; he takes most pleasure in the secret glances of a holy heart. Therefore, a gracious soul prays in secret with the same diligence and care, no, sometimes more, when in a holy frame, that he may reap the comfort of his sincerity before the eyes of God, (Job 31:33).

But no more of this: let us descend to the question deducible from the words, a question of no less importance than daily use, and of peculiar concern to the growth of every Christian.

Chapter 3:
The Duty of Secret Prayer

QUESTION. How to manage secret prayer, that it may be prevalent with God to the comfort and satisfaction of the soul.

For method's sake, I shall divide it into two branches:

1. How to manage secret prayer, that it may prevail with God.

2. How to discern and discover answers to secret prayer, that the soul may acquiesce and be satisfied that it has prevailed with God.

Before I handle these, I would briefly prove the duty and its usefulness, leaving some cases about its attendants and circumstances towards the close.

1. As to the duty itself, the text is plain and distinct in the point. Yet further observe in Solomon's prayer, that if any man besides the community of the people of Israel shall present his supplication to God, he there prays for a gracious and particular answer; (1 Kings 8:38-39; 2 Chron. 6:29-30); and we know Solomon's prayer was answered by fire; (2 Chron. 7:1); and, therefore, here, we may learn a promise given-forth to personal prayer. Besides the many special and particular injunctions to individual persons in the case, as Job 22:27; 33:26; Psalm 32:6; and 50:15, *etc.*; wives, as well as husbands, are to pray "apart," (Zech. 12:14), לְבָד "solitary, alone by themselves," and also consider James 5:13.

We may argue this point from the constant practice of the holy saints of God in all ages, but especially of our blessed Lord; and it is our wisdom to "walk in the way of good men, and keep the paths of the righteous," (Prov. 2:20). What should I speak of Abraham, Eliezer, Isaac, Jacob, Moses, Hannah, Hezekiah, David, and Daniel? The time would fail me to bring-in the cloud of witnesses. Our Lord we find sometimes in a desert, in a mountain, in a garden, at prayer; Cornelius in his house, and Peter upon the house-top, in secret supplications to God. The experience of God's gracious presence and answers sent-in upon secret prayer, as in the stories of Eliezer, Jabez, Nehemiah, Zechariah, Cornelius, and Paul, *etc.*, (1 Chron. 4:10; Neh. 2:4). "For this" cause, because David was heard, "shall every one that is godly pray unto him," (Psalm 32:6).

2. I might urge the usefulness, no, in some cases the necessities, of secret applications to God:

(1). Are we not guilty of secret sins in the light of God's countenance, that cannot, ought not to be, confessed with or before others? Insomuch that near relations are exhorted to secret and solitary duties, (Zech. 12:12; 1 Cor. 7:5).

(2). Are there not personal needs that we would prefer to God alone?

(3). Are there not some special mercies and deliverances that concern our own persons more peculiarly, which should engage us "to commune with our own hearts," and "offer the sacrifices of righteousness" to God? (Psalm 4:4-5).

(4). May there not be found some requests to be poured out more particularly in secret, as to other persons, and as to affairs of the church of God, which may not commodiously be insisted upon in common?

(5). Do not sometimes emergent and urgent passions spring out of the soul in secret, that are not comely in society?

(6). To argue from the text: may not the soul's secret addresses about inward sorrows and joys be a sweet testimony of the sincerity and integrity of the heart, when "the heart knoweth his own bitterness, and a stranger doth not intermeddle with his joy?" (Prov. 14:10). Perhaps a man has an Ishmael, an Absalom, a Rehoboam to weep for, and therefore gets into an inward chamber, (2 Sam. 18:33); where, behold, his "witness is in heaven," and his "record on high," and when others may "scorn" or pity, his "eye poureth out tears unto God," (Job 16:19-20).

To end this: when a holy soul is close in secret, what complacency does it take, when it has bolted out of the world, and retired to a place that no one knows of, to be free from the disturbances and distractions that often violate family communion! When prayer is in the secret of the face of God, in the hidden place of the Most High, and in the shadow of the Almighty, O how safe, how comfortable! (Psalm 31:20; 91:1; Job 29:4).

These and the like I pass by; neither can I insist on secret prayer under the variety of being both mental and vocal; nor enlarge on it as sudden, occasional, or ejaculatory, referring something of this toward the end.

Chapter 4:
Managing Secret Prayer

Let us address, then, the first question: in answer to which I must preface, that some things which aptly belong to secret prayer, yet being in some measure coincident with all prayer, public, private, and secret, it is congruous to treat of such as are of great use as to the management of our present duty; and therefore must refer to a double head.

QUESTION 1. How to manage secret prayer, as it is coincident with prayer in general, so that it may prevail?

1. Use some preparation before it; do not rush suddenly into the awful presence of God. Sanctuary-preparation is necessary to sanctuary-communion. Such suitable preparatory frames of the heart come down from God, "Thou wilt prepare their heart, thou wilt cause thine ear to hear," (Psalm 10:17). It was a good saying of one, *Intimè et devotè nunquam mens orat, quæ se, etc., præmeditationibus prius non excitat.* "He never prays ardently that does not premeditate savorly." Daniel, when he made his famous prayer, it is said he "set" his "face to seek" the Lord, (Dan. 9:3). Jehoshaphat also "set himself to seek the Lord." (2 Chron. 20:3). The church in her soul desires the Lord in the night, and then with her spirit seeks him early, (Isa. 26:9). Desires blown by meditation are the sparks that set prayer in a light flame.

The work of preparation may be cast under five heads, when we apply to solemn and set prayer:

(1). The consideration of some attributes in God that are proper to the intended petitions.

(2). A digestion of some peculiar and special promises that concern the affair.

(3). Meditation on suitable arguments.

(4). Ejaculations for assistance.

(5). An engagement of the heart to a holy frame of reverence and keeping to the point in hand. *Nec quicquam tunc animus quam solum cogitet, quod precatur*, was serious advice from Cyprian: "Let the soul think upon nothing but what it is to pray for;" and he adds that therefore the ministers of old prepared the minds of the people with, *Sursum corda*, "Let your hearts be *above*." For how can we expect to be heard of God, when we do not hear ourselves, when the heart does not watch while the tongue utters? The tongue must be like "the pen of a ready writer," to set down the good matter which the heart composes, (Psalm 45:1). Take heed of ramblings; to preach, or tell pious stories, while praying to the great and holy God, is a branch of irreverence, and a careless frame of spirit, (Heb. 12:28).

2. Humble confession of such sins as concern and refer principally to the work in hand. Our filthy garments must be taken away, when we appear before the Lord that has chosen Jerusalem, (Zech. 3:4). "Look upon mine affliction and my pain," David cried, "and forgive all my sins," (Psalm 25:18). There are certain sins

that often relate to afflictions. First, "Deliver me from all my transgressions;" then, "Hear my prayer, O Lord;" (Psalm 39:8, 12); for this is the heavenly method: he first "forgiveth all" our "iniquities," and then "healeth all" our "diseases," (Psalm 103:3). A forgiven soul is a healed soul. While a man is sick at heart with the qualms of sin unpardoned, it keeps the soul under swooning-fits, that it cannot cry strongly to God, and therefore, in holy groans, he must discharge himself of particular sins, and pour out his soul before God. In this way David did this in that great penitential psalm, Psalm 51:4. For sin like a thick cloud hides the face of God, that our prayers cannot enter, (Isa. 59:2). We must blush with Ezra, (9:6), and our faces look red with the flushing's of conscience, if we expect any smiles of mercy. Our crimson sins must dye our confessions; and the blood of our sacrifices must sprinkle the horns of the golden altar, before we receive an answer of peace from the golden mercy-seat. When our persons are pardoned, our suits are accepted, and our petitions crowned with the olive-branch of peace.

3. Have an arguing and pleading spirit in prayer. This is properly wrestling with God, humble, yet earnest, expostulations about his mind towards us, "Why hast thou cast us off for ever? why doth thine anger smoke?" (Psalm 74:1). "Be not wroth very sore, O Lord, neither remember iniquity for ever: behold, see, we beseech thee, we are all thy people," (Isa. 64:9). "If it be so, why am I thus?" as frightened Rebekah flies out into

prayer, (Gen. 25:22). An arguing frame in prayer cures and appeases the frights of spirit, and then inquires of God, (Psalm 34:4). The temple of prayer is called the soul's inquiring-place, (Psalm 27:4). "Why is God so far from the words of my roaring? You have heard me from the horns of the unicorns." (Psalm 22:1, 21). "How long wilt thou be angry against the prayer of thy people? Turn us again, and cause thy face to shine upon us," (Psalm 80:3-4). "O the hope of Israel, why shouldest thou be as a wayfaring man, as a man astonied? Yet thou, O Lord, art in the midst of us, and we are called by thy name; leave us not," (Jer. 14:8-9). I must refer to Abraham, Jacob, and Moses, Joshua, David, and Daniel, how they urged arguments with God: sometimes from the multitudes of God's mercies, (Psalm 5:7; 6:4; 31:16), from the experience of former answers, from the name of God, (Psalm 4:1; 6:9; 22:4, 21; 31:2, 3, 7; 140:7), from their trust and reliance upon him, (Psalm 9:10; 16:1), from the equity of God, (Psalm 17:1), from the shame and confusion of face that God will put his people to, if not answered, and that others will be driven away from God, (Psalm 31:17; 34:5), and, lastly, from the promise of praise, (Psalm 20:5; 35:18). These and many like pleadings we find in scripture, for patterns in prayer; which, being suggested by the Spirit, kindled from the altar, and perfumed with Christ's incense, rise-up like memorial-pillars before the oracle.

    Let us observe one or two particular prayers, what instant arguments holy men have used and pressed in their perplexities. Jehoshaphat, what a working prayer he made! He took pleas from God's covenant, dominion, and powerful strength; from his gift of the land of Canaan, and driving out the old inhabitants,—ancient mercies! From his sanctuary, and his promise to Solomon; from the ingratitude and ill requital of the enemies; with an appeal to God's equity in the case, and a humble confession of their own impotency, and yet that, in their anxiety, their eyes are fixed upon God, (2 Chron. 20:6–12). You know how gloriously it prevailed, when he had set ambushes round about the court of heaven, and the Lord turned his arguments into ambushes against the children of Edom, *etc.*, (verse 22). Yes, this is set as an instance how God will deal against the enemies of his church in the latter days, (Joel 3:2).

Another is that admirable prayer of the Angel of the covenant to God for the restoration of Jerusalem, wherein he pleads from the length of time and the duration of his indignation for threescore and ten years, from promised mercies and the expiration of prophecies: (Zech. 1:12). And behold an answer of good and comfortable words from the Lord; and I pray that you observe, that when arguments in prayer are very cogent on a sanctified heart, such prayers being drawn from the divine attributes, from precious promises, and sweet experiments of God's former love, it is a rare sign of a prevailing prayer. It was an ingenious passage of Chrysostom concerning the woman of Canaan, Φιλοσοφει ἡ γυνη the poor distressed creature "was turned into an acute philosopher" with Christ, and disputed the mercy from him. O, it is a blessed thing to attain to this heavenly philosophy of prayer, to argue blessings out of the hand of God. Here is a spacious field.

I have given but a small prospect, where the soul, like Jacob, does in *arenam descendere*, "enter the lists" with omnipotence, and by holy force obtain the blessing.

4. Ardent affections in prayer, showing a heart deeply sensible, are greatly prevalent. A crying prayer pierces the depths of heaven. We do not read a word that Moses spoke, but God was moved by his cry, (Exod. 14:15). I do not mean a disruptive noise, but melting moans of heart. Yet sometimes the sore and pinching necessities and distresses of spirit extort even vocal cries which are not unpleasant to the inclined ears of God. "I cried unto the Lord with my voice," David says, "and he heard me out of his holy hill," (Psalm 3:4). And this encourages to a fresh onset, "Hearken unto the voice of my cry, my King, and my God," (Psalm 5:2). "Give ear unto my cry; hold not thy peace at my tears," (Psalm 39:12). Another time he makes the cave echo with his cries, "I cried, I cried. Attend unto my cry; for I am brought very low." And what is the issue? Faith gets courage by crying. His tears watered his faith that it grew into confidence, and so concludes, "Thou shalt deal bountifully with me, and the righteous shall crown me for conqueror," (Psalm 142:1, 5–7). Plentiful tears bring bountiful mercies, and a crying suitor proves a triumphant praiser.

Holy Jacob was just such another: at the fords of Jabbok he prevailed with the Angel, for "he wept, and made supplication unto him," (Hosea 12:4). Hezekiah may bring up the rear: for the Lord told him he had heard his prayer, for he had seen his tears, (2 Kings 20:5). Such precedents may well encourage backsliding Ephraim to return and bemoan himself; and then the "bowels" of God "are troubled for him," (Jer. 31:18–20). No, we have a holy woman likewise weeping sorely before the Lord in Shiloh, and then rejoicing in his salvation, (1 Sam. 1:10; 2:1). The cries of saints are like vocal music joined with the instrument of prayer; they make heavenly melody in the ears of God. The bridegroom calls to his mourning dove, "Let me hear thy voice;' for that is pleasant," (Song of Songs 2:14). What Gerson says of the sores of Lazarus, *Quot vulnera, tot linguas habuit*, "As many wounds, so many tongues," we may say of sighs, cries, and groans in prayer, "So many eloquent orators at the throne of God."

5. Importunity and assiduity in prayer is highly prevalent. *Non ut fastidiosa continuetur oratio, sed ut assidua frequenter effundatur.* "Not that we should lengthen out prayer with tedious and vain repetitions," as the heathen did of old, (Matt. 6:7), or as the Euchitæ in Constantius' time, that did little else but pray, "but that we should be frequent, and continue incessantly, in prayer." Whereas our Lord bids us to "pray always," (Luke 18:1), and the apostle Paul tells us to "pray without ceasing," (1 Thess. 5:17). We are to understand it of being constant at times every day. As the morning and evening

sacrifice at the temple is called the "continual burnt-offering," (Num. 28:4, 6), as Mephibosheth is said to "eat bread continually," at David's table, (2 Sam. 9:7), and Solomon's servants to stand continually before him, that is, at the set and appointed times, so it is required of us to be constant and assiduous at prayer, and to follow our lawful requests with perseverance. In this way, Hannah is said to "multiply prayer," (1 Sam. 1:12), and received multiplied answers; expressly indeed she prayed but for one son, but she had six children returned-in on her prayer.

When the soul perseveres in prayer, it is a sign of a persevering faith; and such may have what they will at the hand of God, when praying according to prescript, (John 16:23). No, urgent prayer is the token of a mercy at hand. When Elijah prayed seven times one after another for rain, the clouds presently march up out of the sea at the command of prayer, (1 Kings 18:43, 44). "Ask of me things to come," the Lord says, "and concerning the work of my hands command ye me," (Isa. 45:11). When we put forth our utmost strength in prayer, and will, as it were, do not receive a "no" from heaven, our prayers must be like the continual blowing of the silver trumpets over the sacrifices "for a memorial before the Lord," (Num. 10:10); like the watchmen on the walls of Jerusalem, who "never hold their peace day nor night," and are commanded "not to keep silence, nor to give him rest," (Isa. 62:6-7). No, God seems offended at other times, that they did not lay hands on him, that they might not be consumed in their iniquities, (Isa. 64:7). Such prayers are, as it were, a holy molestation to the throne of grace.

It is said of the man that rose at midnight to give out three loaves to his friend, he did not do it for friendship's sake, but δια την αναιδειαν, "because he was impudent," so importunately to trouble him at such a season as twelve o'clock at night, (Luke 11:8). Our Lord applies the parable to instant prayers. The same we find of the success of the widow with the unjust judge, because she did ὦαρεχειν κοπον, "vex and molest" him with her solicitations, (Luke 18:5). But of all, the pattern of the woman of Canaan is most admirable, when the disciples desired her to be dismissed, because she troubled them by crying after them, and yet she persists, (Matt. 15:23). May I say it reverently? Christ delights in such a troublesome person. Though, as an ancient observes, by comparing both evangelists, that first she cried after Christ in the streets, (Matt. 15:22), but our Lord going into the house, she follows him there, and falls down at his feet; (Mark 7:24, 25); but as yet he "answered her not a word." (Matt. 15:23:) In *eo silentio egressum fuisse Jesum de domo illâ,* then our Lord going out of the house again, she follows with stronger importunity, and argues the mercy into her bosom, and Christ ascribes it to the greatness of her faith; καλη αναισχυντια, as another describes it, "a laudable and praiseworthy immodesty;" as, in the former case, to knock so rudely at midnight is deemed no incivility at the gate of heaven. This is δεησις ενεργουμενη as Guil. Parisiensis reads it, *deprecatio justi assidua,* (James 5:16). "An assiduous prayer" is the way to become "an efficacious prayer." It is ill taken, if not importunate. Cold petitioners must have cool answers from God. If the matter of prayer is right, and the promise of God fervently urged, you are likely to prevail like princely Israel, that held the Angel by the collar, (to speak with reverence), and would not let him go until he had blessed him. But it was hot work most of the night, even to break of day, (Gen. 32:24–26); to show that in some cases of extremity we must hold out in prayers. For our Lord in the next verse to the text does not forbid the length of prayer, for he himself upon occasion continues a whole night in prayer; (Luke 6:12); but he forbids such as are filled with impertinent multiplications of vain words, and have neither holy reasonings nor spiritual and warm affections, and yet think to be "heard for their much speaking."

QUESTION. "But can God be moved by our arguments, or affected with our troubles? He is the unchangeable God, and dwells in the inaccessible light. There "is no variableness, neither shadow of turning," (James 1:17), which is a metaphor from the fixed stars, which allow no parallax, and therefore astronomers cannot demonstrate their magnitude. For our eyes or instruments can yet give no intelligence of any increase or diminution of their diameter or light.

ANSWER. Those holy motions on the hearts of saints in prayer are the fruits of the unchangeable decrees of his love to them, and the appointed ushers of mercy. God graciously determines to give a praying, arguing, warm, affectionate frame, as the *prodromus* and "forerunner" of a decreed mercy. That is the reason that carnal men can enjoy no such mercies, because they pour out no such prayers. The spirit of prayer prognosticates mercy ensuing. Therefore, when the Lord by Jeremiah foretold the end of the captivity, he also pre-signifies the prayers that should open the gates of Babylon, (Jer. 29:10, 12). Cyrus was prophesied of, to do his work for Jacob his servant's sake and Israel his elect; but yet they must ask him concerning those things to come, and they should not seek him in vain, (Isa. 45:1-2, 4, 11, 19). The glory of the latter days in the return of Israel is foretold by Ezekiel; but yet then the Lord "will be inquired of by the house of Israel, to do it for them," (Ezek. 36:24, 37). The coming of Christ is promised by himself; but yet "the Spirit and the bride say, Come;" and he "that heareth" must "say, Come." And when Christ says he will "come quickly." "Even so, come, Lord Jesus." (Rev. 22:12, 17, 20). Divine grace kindles these ardent affections, when the mercies promised are flying "upon the wing." Prayer is that intelligible chain, as Dionysius calls it, that draws the souls up to God, and the mercy down to us; or like the cable that draws the ship to land, though the shore itself remains unmovable. Prayer has its kindling's from heaven, like the ancient sacrifices that were inflamed with celestial fire, (2 Chron. 7:1).

6. Submission to the all-wise and holy will of God. This is the great benefit of a saint's communion with the Spirit, that "He maketh intercession for" them "according to the will of God," (Rom. 8:27). When promised mercies are revealed in more absolute terms, the sanctified will concenters with the will of God. When we pray for holiness, there is a concurrence with the divine will, "For this is the will of God, even your sanctification," (1 Thess. 4:3). When we pray that our bodies may be presented "a living sacrifice, acceptable unto God," we then "prove what is that good, and acceptable, and perfect will of God," (Rom. 12:1-2). But I speak here as to outward mercies and enjoyments, and the degrees of graces and spiritual mercies. But as to substance of spiritual mercies, the promises in such cases run freely; as, if in any place there seem to lie any limitations or conditions, those very conditions are otherwise graciously promised to be fashioned in us. In the covenant of grace, God does his part and ours too. As, when God commands us to pray in one place, he promises in another place to pour-out upon us "the spirit of grace and of supplications," (Zech. 12:10). God commands us to "repent and turn" to him, (Ezek. 14:6). In another place, "Turn thou me, and I shall be turned; for thou art the Lord my God, (Jer. 31:18); and again, "Turn thou us unto thee, O Lord, and we shall be turned," (Lam. 5:21). "Make you a new heart and a new

spirit," and another place, "A new heart will I give you, and a new spirit will I put within you," *etc.*, "and cause you to walk in my statutes," (Ezek. 18:31; 36:26-27). "That ye might walk unto all pleasing," Paul says, "for this cause we do not cease to pray for you," *etc.*, (Col. 1:9, 10); that he would "work in you that which is well-pleasing in his sight," (Heb. 13:21). "Work out your own salvation. For it is God which worketh in you both to will and to do of his good pleasure," (Phil. 2:12-13). Precepts, promises, and prayer, are connected, like so many golden links, to excite, encourage, and assist the soul in spiritual duties. But in other cases, as to temporal and temporary mercies, let all your desires in prayer be formed with submission, guided by his counsel, and prostrate at his feet, and acted by a faith suitable to the promises of outward blessings; and then it shall "be unto thee even as thou wilt," (Matt. 15:28). He said well, *Cardo desideriorum sit voluntas Dei; ut exaudiat, pete cardinem,* "Let all thy desires as to temporals turn upon the hinge of the divine good pleasure. That man shall have his own will that resolves to make God's will his." God will certainly bestow that which is for the good of his people, (Psalm 34:17; 84:11; Matt. 7:11; Rom. 8:28). One great point of our mortification lies in this, to have our wills melted into God's; and it is a great token of spiritual growth, when we are not only content, but joyful, to see our wills crossed, that his may be done. We pray that his "kingdom" may "come;" let it appear by sincere prayer that his "will" may "be done." When our wills are sacrificed in the flames of holy prayer, we many times receive choicer things than we ask expressly. It was a good saying, *Non dat quod volumus, ut det quod malimus*, "God many times grants not what we will in the present prayers, that he may bestow what we had rather have," when we have the prayer more graciously answered than we petitioned. We do not know how to pray as we ought, but the Spirit helps us out with groans that secretly hint a correction of our wills and spirit in prayer, (Rom. 8:26). In great anxieties and pinching troubles, nature dictates strong groans for relief; but sustaining grace, and participation of divine holiness, mortification from earthly comforts, (Heb. 12:10), excitation of the soul to long for heaven, being gradually weaned from the wormwood-breasts of these sublunary, transient, and unsatisfying pleasures, and the timing of our hearts for the seasons, in which God will time his deliverances, are sweeter mercies than the present return of a prayer for an outward good into our bosoms. What truly holy person would lose that "light of" God's "countenance," which he enjoyed by glimpses in a cloudy day, for a little "corn and wine?" "You have put more gladness into my heart," David says, (Psalm 4:6-7). No, in many cases open denials of prayer prove out the most excellent answers, and God's not hearing us is the most signal audience. Therefore, at the foot of every prayer subscribe, *Fiat voluntas tua*, "Thy will be done," and you shall enjoy preventing mercies that you never looked for, and converting mercies to change everything for the best; resting confident in this, that having asked "according to his will, he heareth" thee, (1 John 5:14).

7. Lastly. Present everything into the hands of Christ. This was signified of old by praying toward the temple, (1 Kings 8:33), because the golden mercy-seat, typifying Christ, was there. He is "ordained" of God "to offer gifts and sacrifices;" and therefore it is of necessity that he should have something from us to offer, being the "high priest over the house of God," (Heb. 8:3; 10:21). What does Christ do on our behalf at the throne of grace? Put some petition into the hands of Christ; he waits for our offerings at the door of the oracle; leave the sighs and groans of your heart with this compassionate Intercessor, who is "touched with the feeling of our infirmities," (Heb. 4:15), who sympathizes with our weaknesses. He that lies in the Father's bosom, and has "expounded," εξηγησατο, the will of God to us, (John 1:18), adds a great amount of incense to "the prayers of all saints before the throne" of God, and explains our wills to God; (Rev. 8:3). Our prayers, perfumed by his, are "set forth as incense before" him, (Psalm 141:2). He is the "days-man," (Job 9:33), the heavens-man between God and us. Whatever we ask in his name, he puts into his golden censer, that the Father may give it to us, (John 15:16; 16:23). When the sweet smoke of the incense of Christ's prayer ascends before the Father, our prayers become sweet and amiable, and cause "a savour of rest" with God, (Gen. 8:21). This I take to be one reason why the prevalence of prayer is so often assigned to the time

of the evening sacrifice, pointing at the death of Christ, "about the ninth hour" of the day, near the time of the evening oblation, (Matt. 27:46; Acts 3:1; 10:30). It was here that Abraham's sacrifice received a gracious answer, being offered about the going down of the sun, (Gen. 15:12). Isaac went out to pray "at eventide." (Gen. 24:63). Elijah, at mount Carmel, prays and offers "at the time of the evening sacrifice." (1 Kings 18:36). Ezra "fell upon" his "knees, and spread out" his "hands, at the evening sacrifice," (Ezra 9:5). David begs that his prayer may be virtual in the power of "the evening sacrifice." (Psalm 141:2). Daniel, at prayer, was touched by the angel "about the time of the evening oblation," (Dan. 9:21). All to show the prevalence of our access to the throne of grace by the virtuous merit of the intercession of Christ, the acceptable evening Sacrifice. Yes, and therefore we are taught in our Lord's prayer to begin with the title of "Father:" in him we are adopted to children, and to use that prevalent relation as an argument in prayer. There are some other particulars in respect to prayer in general, as it may be connected and coincident with secret prayer, as stability of spirit, freedom from distraction by wandering thoughts, the acts of faith, the aids of the Spirit, *etc.*, which I pass by, and come to the second branch.

Chapter 5:
Directions for Secret Prayer

1. Be sure of having an intimate acquaintance with God. Can we presume, that are but dust and ashes, to go up into heaven, and boldly to enter the presence-chamber, and have no fellowship with the Father, or with the Son? "Acquaint now thyself with him, and be at peace," *etc.* "Then shalt thou have thy delight in the Almighty, and shalt lift up thy face unto God. Thou shalt make thy prayer unto him, and he shall hear thee." The decrees of your heart "shall be established unto thee: and the light shall shine upon thy ways," (Job 22:21, 26–28).

First shining acquaintance, and then shining answers, (Job 29:3-4). Can you set your face to the Lord God? Then you may seek him by prayer. First Daniel sets and shows his face to God, and then seeks him "by prayer and supplications," (Dan. 9:3). Does God know your face in prayer? Do you often converse in your closets with him? Believe it, it must be the fruit of intimate acquaintance with God, to meet him in secret *with delight.* Can ye come familiarly, as a child to a father, considering its own vileness, meanness, or unworthiness, in comparison with his divine love, the love and bowels of a heavenly Father? Such a Father, the Father of fathers, and the Father of mercies! How sweetly does the apostle join it! God is "our Father" because "the Father of our Lord;" and because his Father, and so our Father, therefore "the Father of mercies," (2

Cor. 1:2-3). O! what generations of mercies flow from this paternity! But plead we must to that ὦροσαγωγη, that "manuduction and access" to this Father through Christ by the Spirit, (Eph. 2:18). We must be gradually acquainted with all Three. First with the Spirit, then with Christ, and last with the Father: first God sends "the Spirit of his Son into our hearts," and then through the Son we cry, "Abba, Father." (Gal. 4:6). The bowels of mercy first fashioned in the Father to us, He chose us in Christ, and then sends his Spirit to draw us to Christ, and by Christ to himself, (Eph. 1:4-5). Do you have this access to God by the Spirit? Heart-communion flows from heart-affection. If your souls are truly in love with God, he will graciously say to your petitions, "Be it unto you according to your love."

2. Times of finding God. A godly man prays in finding seasons; when God's heart and ear are inclined to audience, when God is said to "bow down" his "ear unto" us, (Psalm 31:2). There are special seasons of drawing near to him, when he draws near to us, times when he "may be found," (Isa. 55:6; Psalm 32:6). When your "beloved looketh forth at the windows, showing himself through the lattice," that is a time of grace, when he knocks at the door of thy heart by his Spirit, (Song of Songs 2:9; 5:2). Motions on the heart are like the doves of the East sent with letters around their necks; as he said of Bernard, *Ex motu cordis Spiritûs Sancti præsentiam agnoscebat,* "He knew when the Holy Spirit was present with him, by the motion of his heart." When

God reveals himself to the heart, he opens the ears of his servants for some gracious message, (2 Sam. 7:27). When God bids us "seek his face," then the soul must answer, "One thing have I desired, that will I seek after," (Psalm 27:4, 8). First holy desires warm the heart, and then set the soul on seeking. They are like messengers sent from heaven to bring us into his presence. Take heed, then, of quenching the Spirit of God. He "that is born of the Spirit" knows "the sound," φωνην, "the voice of the Spirit," (John 3:8). When the soul is melted by the word, or softened by afflictions, or feels some holy groans and sighs excited by the Spirit, that is a warm time for prayer; then we enjoy "the sense," το φρονημα του Πνευματος, "the intimations of the Spirit of God," (Rom. 8:27). Or when prophecies are ready to expire, then there are great workings and searchings of heart in Daniel, Zachariah, Simeon, and Anna. Or when some promise comes with applying power, "Therefore hath thy servant found in his heart to pray this prayer unto thee;" for "you have promised this goodness unto thy servant," (2 Sam. 7:2-28). When we find promises dropped into the soul like wine, it causes "the lips of" them that were "asleep to speak," (Song of Songs 7:9).

3. Keep conscience tender of, and clean from, secret sins. With what face can we go to a friend to whom we have given any secret affronts? And will you be so bold as to come before the God of heaven, when he knows you maintain some secret lust in your heart? Dare you to bring a Delilah with you into this sacred closet? It

is true that of Tertullian, *Quantum a præceptis, tantum ab auribus Dei longè sumus.* He that turns his ear from God's precepts, must stop his mouth in the dust, if God turn his holy ears from his cries, (Prov. 28:9). When our secret sins are in the light of his countenance, we may rather expect to be "consumed by" his "anger, and troubled by" his "wrath." (Psalm 90:7-8).

OBJECTION. "But, then, who may presume and venture into secret communion?"

ANSWER. True, if God should strictly mark what we do amiss, who can stand? David was sensible of this objection, but he answers it humbly, "There is forgiveness with thee, that thou mayest be feared." (Psalm 130:3-4). If we come with holy purposes to leave all sin, he has promised to "pardon abundantly." His thoughts and ways are not as ours, (Isa. 55:7-8). Guilt makes us fly from his presence; but proclamation of pardoning grace to a wounded soul that comes for strength from heaven to subdue its iniquities, sweetly draws the soul to lie at his foot for mercy, (Micah 7:19). Though we cannot as yet be so free as formerly, while under the wounding sense of guilt, yet when he "restores to" us "the joy of his salvation," he will again "uphold" us with his "free Spirit," (Psalm 51:12). Yet take heed of scars upon the soul. God "knows our foolishness; and our guiltinesses are not hid from him," (Psalm 69:5); yet we come for purging and cleansing mercy. A godly man may be under the sense of divine displeasure, for some iniquity of himself knows, as the Lord spoke of Eli; (1

Sam. 3:13); yet the way to be cured is not to run from God, but, like the distressed woman, come fearing and trembling, and fall at his feet, and tell him all the truth, (Mark 5:33). But if prayer has cured you, sin no more, lest a worse thing come to you. For if we "regard iniquity in" our "heart, the Lord will not hear" us, (Psalm 66:18); but the guilt may stare conscience in the face with great amazement. As it is storied of one that secretly had stolen a sheep, it ran before his eyes in prayer so that he could have no rest. How strangely will memory ring the bell in the ears of conscience! If we have any secret sin *in deliciis*, if we look but asquint with desires and secret thoughts, after our "peace-offerings," (Prov. 7:14), to meet our "beloved lusts" again, *this is dangerous*. God may justly give-up such to cast off that which is good, to cleave to their idols, and let them alone, (Hosea 4:17; 6:4). But if the face of the heart is not knowingly and willingly spotted with any sin or lust, bating infirmities which he mourns under, then your countenance through Christ will be comely in the eye of God, and your voice sweet in his ears; and as he said, *Qui benè vivit, semper orat,* "A holy life will be a walking of continual prayer; his very life is a constant petition before God."

  4. Own your personal interest with God, and plead it humbly. Consider whom you go to in secret. "Pray to thy Father who seeth in secret." Can you prove yourself to be in covenant? What you can prove you may plead, and have it successfully issued. In prayer we take God's covenant into our mouths, but without a real

interest. The Lord expostulates with such, What have they "to do with" it? (Psalm 50:15-16). God never graciously hears except it comes to him on interest. This argument Solomon presses in prayer, "For they be thy people, and thine inheritance," (1 Kings 8:51). In this way David pleads, "Thou art my God: hear the voice of my supplications," (Psalm 140:6). "I am thine," Lord, "save me," (Psalm 119:94). "Truly I am thy servant; I am thy servant," (Psalm 116:16). Arias turns אָנָּה by *obsecro, quæso*, "I beseech thee, O Lord, I am thy servant." God will "avenge his elect" when they cry to him, "I was cast upon thee from the womb: thou art my God from my mother's belly," (Luke 18:7; Psalm 22:10). Therefore, Asa turns the contest heavenward, "O Lord, thou art our God; let not mortal man prevail against thee," (2 Chron. 14:11). "Thou takest me for the 'sheep' of thy fold, and the 'servant' of thy household; therefore 'seek' me," (Psalm 119:176). When Israel shall be refined as silver and tried as gold, "they shall call on" his "name, and" he "will hear them: I will say, It is my people," my tried, refined, golden people: "and they shall say, The Lord is my God," (Zech. 13:9). When you can discern the print of the broad seal of the covenant on your heart, and the privy-seal of the Spirit upon your prayers, and can look on the Son of God in a sacerdotal relation to you, you may "come boldly unto the throne of grace in time of need," (Heb. 4:16).

    5. Be very particular in secret prayer, both as to sins, wants, and mercies, (Psalm 32:5; 51:9). Do not hide

Chapter 5: Directions for Secret Prayer

any of your transgressions, if you expect a pardon. Do not be ashamed to open all your necessities. David argues, because he is "poor and needy;" several times (four times) he presses his needs and exigences before God, like an earnest but holy beggar, (Psalm 40:17; 70:5; 86:1; 109:22); and "showed before him" his "trouble," (Psalm 142:2), from נֶגֶד, *coram*, which means he presents "before" him his ragged condition, and spreads open his secret wounds. Job said, he "would order" his "cause before him," (Job 23:4), from עָרַךְ, *disponerem*, *instruerem*, meaning "marshal" every case as a battle in rank and file. There we may speak out our minds fully, and name the persons that afflict, affront, and trouble us; and woe to them that a child of God on a mature judgment names in prayer! I do not find that such a prayer in scripture returned empty. Jacob, in a great strait, says, "Deliver me from the hand of my brother, from the hand of Esau" (Gen. 32:11). David, in the ascent of Mount Olivet, "O Lord, I pray thee, turn the counsel of Ahithophel into foolishness." Prayer twisted the rope for him at Giloh, (2 Sam. 15:12, 31; 17:23). In this way, Jehoshaphat in his prayer names Ammon, Moab, and Edom conspiring against him, (2 Chron. 20:10). In this way, Hezekiah spreads the railing letter before the Lord, (Isa. 37:14); and the Psalmist takes them all in a round catalogue that consulted against Israel, (Psalm 83:5–8). In this way, the church in her prayer names Herod Antipas and Pontius Pilate (Acts 4:27); of which the first was sent into perpetual banishment, and the latter killed himself. It is of great use in prayer to attend to some special case or single request with arguments and affections suitable. "For this cause," Paul says, "I bow my knees." (Eph. 3:14). Suppose a grace deficient in its strength, "Lord, increase our faith;" (Luke 17:5); or a temptation urgent: "For this thing I besought the Lord thrice, that it might depart from me," (2 Cor. 12:8). A great reason why we reap so little benefit by prayer is, because we rest too much in generals; and if we have success, it is but dark, so that often we cannot tell what to make of the issues of prayer. Besides, to be particular in our petitions would keep the spirit much from wandering, when we are intent upon a weighty case, and the progress of the soul in grace would manifest its gradual success in prayer.

6. Holy and humble appeals before the Lord in secret, when the soul can submissively and thankfully expose itself to divine searching about some measures of holiness and grace fashioned in the heart. The soul cannot abide by the presence of God under flashings of defilement; *neque agnosci poterit a Spiritu Sancto spiritus inquinatus,* "neither will the Holy Spirit own a defiled soul." But when a person can humbly, modestly, and reverently say, "Search me, and try my reins; and see if there be any way of wickedness in me, and lead me in the everlasting way," (Psalm 26:2; 139:23, 24); it will be the means of the sudden outburst of emotions and boilings-up of joyful affections and meek confidence at the footstool of grace, especially in pleas of deliverance

from wicked and proud enemies. When David can plead in comparison with, and in the case stated between, his enemies and himself, "For I am holy," it shows him "a token for good," (Psalm 86:2, 14, 17). Or when we plead against the assaults of Satan, can we be conscious that we have watched and prayed against entering into temptation? When we can "wash" our "hands in innocency," we may then comfortably compass God's altar about, (Psalm 26:6). In case of opposition and injustice: "He rewarded me," David says, in the point of Saul, "according to my righteousness, and to the cleanness of my hands before him," (Psalm 18:20; 7:3–5). Or about the truth of the love that is in the heart to God, "Thou that knowest all things," Peter says, "knowest that I love thee." (John 21:17). As to zeal for the worship and ordinances of God, so did Nehemiah, (Neh. 13:14, 22). As to the integrity of a well-spent life, so did Hezekiah, (Isa. 38:3). Or if we cannot rise so high, yet we may say as the church did, "The desire of our soul is to thy name, and to the remembrance of thee," (Isa. 26:8). Or, lastly, when we can unfeignedly plead the usefulness of a mercy entreated, in order to the divine glory; as when a minister, or the church of Christ for him, prays for such gifts and graces, such knowledge and "utterance," that he may win souls to Christ, and can appeal that it is his principal aim; (Eph. 6:19; Col. 4:3); this is glorious.

7. Pray for the Spirit, that you may pray in and by the Spirit. Awaken the north and the south to "blow

upon thy garden, that the spices thereof may flow forth." Then you may invite Christ, "Let my beloved come into his garden, and eat his pleasant fruits," (Song of Songs 4:16); that the soul may enjoy him and hold sweet communion with him. All successful prayer is from the breathing of the Spirit of God, when he inspires and composes, when he directs the heart as to matter, and governs the tongue as to utterance, (1 Cor. 2:13). God graciously hears the sighs of his own Spirit formed in us, (Rom. 8:26-27). He sent forth his Spirit, "and the waters flow," (Psalm 147:18). That I may allude: the waters of contrition flow upon the breathing of the Spirit; and the soul is, as it were, all afloat before the throne of grace, when these living waters issue from under the threshold of the sanctuary, (Ezek. 47:1). *Sequitur lachrymosa devotio flante Spiritu Sancto,* "Devout tears drop down from the Spirit's influences." Melting supplications follow the infusions of grace by the Spirit. Then "they shall mourn for" piercing of Christ, the prophet says, "and shall be in bitterness, as for a first-born: like the mourning at the town of Hadadrimmon," where Josiah was slain, (Zech. 12:10-11). Then, "in that day," what inundations of mercy shall refresh the church, when the Lord "will extend her peace like a river, and the glory of the Gentiles like a flowing stream;" great things to the church, and gracious things to the soul! (Isa. 66:12; Zech. 13:1, 2, 4; 14:8). *Inter orationem suspiria cognoscit,* "Holy sighs in prayer give intelligence of great mercies to follow." No, to withstand powerfully all the wiles of

Satan, one means is, to consecrate every part of the spiritual armor by "prayer in the Spirit," (Eph. 6:18).

8. Apply special promises to special cases in prayer. "For God hath magnified" and will magnify his "word" of promise "above all his name," (Psalm 138:2). When we are under the word of command for a duty, we must seek for a word of promise, and unite them in prayer, (John 12:28). When a promise of aid suits to the precept, it renders prayer victorious, and obedience pleasant. When we come with God's own words into his presence, when we take his words with us that he would "take away all iniquity," he will "receive us graciously," (Hosea 14:2). Jacob urged that God had bid him return unto his country and kindred, (Gen. 32:9). Solomon urges the word of promise to David, (1 Kings 8:24). Jehoshaphat urges the word of promise to Solomon, (2 Chron. 20:8, 9). Daniel fills his mouth with the promise given to Jeremiah; he reads, and then applies it in prayer, (Dan. 9:2-3). First, search the Bible, and look for a promise, and when found, open it before the Lord. Paul teaches us to take the promise given to Joshua, and then to "say boldly, The Lord is our helper," *etc.*, (Heb. 13:5-6). For the special ground of the answer of prayer lies in the performance of a promise, (Psalm 50:15; 65:2, 4). Simeon *lived* on a promise, and expired sweetly in the arms of a promise in the breathings of a prayer, (Luke 2:29). Sometimes the soul depends for an answer by virtue of the covenant in general; as of that, "I will be thy God," (Gen. 17:7-8); sometimes, by the great

Remembrancer, "draws water out of some well of salvation," (John 14:26; Isa. 12:3:) but in both, God's faithfulness is the soul's surety. It is here that David in prayer does so often argue upon the veracity and truth of God; and the church, in Micah, is so confident that "the mercy" promised "to Abraham, and confirmed in truth to Jacob," should be plentifully performed to his people Israel, (Micah 7:20).

9. Have sober and serious resolutions before God in prayer. Psalm 119 is full of these, "I will keep thy statutes." (Verse 8). "I will run the way of thy commandments." (Verse 32). "I will speak of thy testimonies before kings." (Verse 46). "I have sworn, and I will perform it, that I will keep thy righteous judgments." (Verse 106). And other-where: "Quicken us, and we will call upon thy name." (Psalm 80:18). And again: "O when wilt thou come unto me? I will walk within my house with a perfect heart." (Psalm 101:2). "Visit me with answers of mercy to prayer;" and then the soul makes holy stipulations and compacts of obedience to God. Jacob did this, "If God will be with me, then shall the Lord be my God;" and resolves upon a house for God, and reserving the tenth of all his estate to his service and worship, (Gen. 28:20–22). Where the particle אִם, *si*, "if," is not to be taken for a single conditional word, as that if God should not bestow what he promised, he should not be his God; that would be a great wickedness. But it is a rational particle, or of order and time. "Because," or, "Since God is graciously pleased to promise, I will

acknowledge him to be the God whom I adore, by erecting a temple, and paying tithes to maintain his worship," (Gen. 35:3). But whatever it is that the soul in distress offers to God in promise, do not be slack to perform; for many times answers of prayer may delay until we have performed our promises, (Eccles. 5:4). David professes to pay what his lips had uttered in trouble; for God had heard him, (Psalm 66:13–19). If we break our words to God, no wonder if we feel what the Lord threatened to Israel, that they should "know his breach of promise," (Num. 14:34).

10. Have a waiting frame of spirit in prayer. "I waited patiently for the Lord; and he inclined unto me, and heard my cry." (Psalm 40:1). קַוֹּה קִוִּיתִי, "I expected with expectation;" he walked up and down in the gallery of prayer. This is set forth by hope until God hears, "In thee, O Lord, do I hope: thou wilt hear, O Lord my God," (Psalm 38:15). "Our eyes" must "wait upon the Lord our God, until he have mercy upon us, more than they that watch for the morning," (Psalm 123:2; 130:6); and persist praying, "Cause us to hear thy loving-kindness in the morning; for in thee do we trust," (Psalm 143:8); and say, with Micah: "I will look unto the Lord; I will wait for the God of my salvation: my God will hear me," (Micah 7:7); hoping, expecting, trusting, living upon the promise, and looking for an answer of peace; as he said of prayer, *Sagitta movetur post quietem sagittantis, et navis quiescentibus nautis,* "When an archer shoots an arrow, he looks after it with his glass, to see how it hits the

mark." So the soul says, "I will attend and watch how my prayer flies towards the bosom of God, and what messages return from heaven." "As the seaman, when he has set sail, goes to the helm and the compass, and sits still" and observes the sun or the pole-stars, and how the ship works, and how the land-marks form themselves aright according to his chart: so do you, when you have been at prayer: mark your ship how it makes the port, and what rich goods are laden back again from heaven. Most men lose their prayers in the mists and fogs of non-observation: and in this way we arrive at the second question.

Chapter 6: Answered Prayer

QUESTION 2. How to discover and discern answers to secret prayer, that the soul may be satisfied that it has prevailed with God.

Let us now consider the αποδοσις, "rendition or reply" to prayer, in the text. He will return it into your hearts. And as to this in general, we look to understand the mercy sought for which is speedily and particularly cast into your arms; like the creatures in nature which in their natural cries seek their meat from God, and gather what he gives them, and "are filled with good," (Psalm 104:28; 147:9). When God openly returns to his children, there is no further dispute. For the worst of men will acknowledge the divine bounty, when he fills their, "hearts with food and gladness," (Acts 14:17).

OBSERVATION 1. But when cases are a little dubious, observe the frame and temper of your spirit in prayer. How the heart works and steers its course can be seen in several particulars:

1. A holy liberty of spirit is commonly an excellent sign of answers, a copious spirit of fluentness to pour out requests as out of a fountain, (2 Cor. 3:17). As God shuts-up opportunities, so he shuts-up hearts, when he is not inclined to hear. The heart is sometimes locked up that it cannot pray; or if it does and will press on, it finds a straightness, as if the Lord had spoken, as once to Moses, "Speak no more unto me of this matter;"

(Deut. 3:26); or as God spake to Ezekiel, "Though Noah, Daniel, and Job" should entreat for a nation, when the time of a land is come, there is no salvation but for "their own souls," (Ezek. 14:14; 7:2, 7, 11). When God intends to take away near relations or any of his saints to himself, many times neither the church of God nor dear friends have either apt seasons or hearts to enlarge; the bow of prayer does not abide in strength. God took away gracious Josiah suddenly. The church had time to write a book of Lamentations, and to make it "an ordinance in Israel," but no time for deprecation of the divine displeasure in it, (2 Chron. 35:25). But in Hezekiah's case there was both a season and a heart enlarged in prayer, and the prophet crying for a sign of the mercy, (2 Kings 20:11). Holy James might be quickly dispatched by the sword of Herod Agrippa; but the church had time for supplication in behalf of Peter, (Acts 12:2, 12). When the Lord is pleased graciously to grant space of time and enlargement of heart, it is a notable sign of success. "You have enlarged me when I was in distress," David says, (Psalm 4:1). Though it is meant of deliverance, yet it may be applied to prayer, as the holy prophet seems to do. Yes, though the soul may be under some sense of displeasure and in extremities, yet it lifts up a cry, (Psalm 18:6); when conscience stops the mouth of hypocrites, they shun and fly from the presence of God.

  2. Have a blessed serenity and quiet calmness of spirit in time of prayer. Especially when the soul comes troubled and clouded at first, while it poured out its

complaints before the Lord; but at length, *nescio quid serenius emicat, etc.*, "the sun shines forth brightly, and the heavens look serenely and cheerfully upon the soul in prayer." It is said of Hannah, she "was no more sad," Hebrew, "her countenance was not," לָהּ עוֹד *illi ulterius,* "any longer in the old hue," cast down and sorrowful because of her rival, (1 Sam. 1:18). In this way, the Lord dealt with David, though not yet fully answered, yet filled with holy fortitude of spirit, and "revived in the midst of "his "trouble," (Psalm 138:3, 7). Prayer dispels anxious solicitude, and chases away black thoughts from the heart; it eases the conscience, and fills the soul with "the peace of God," (Phil. 4:6-7).

    3. A joyful frame of spirit. God sometimes makes his people not only peaceful but "joyful in" his "house of prayer," (Isa. 56:7). In this way, Hezekiah sped, when his crane-like chattering's were turned into swan-like songs, and his mournful elegies into glorious praises upon ten-stringed "instruments in the house of the Lord," (Isa. 38:14, 20). The "lips" of Habakkuk "quivered," and his "belly trembled;" but before he finished, his voice was talkative in holy songs, and his fingers nimble on the harp, (Hab. 3:16, 19). In this way, at Solomon's prayer, the fire came down, the people were warmed at worship, and went away "glad and merry at heart." (2 Chron. 7:1, 10). David's experience of this sent him often to the house of God for comfort; and he in this way chides his soul when cast down at any time, "I am going to the altar of God; unto God my

exceeding joy. Why art thou disquieted within me?" (Psalm 43:4-5). His old harp, that had cured Saul of his malignant dumps, being played upon with temple-songs, now cures his own spiritual sadness. When we look upon God with an eye of faith in prayers, it "enlightens" our faces with heavenly joy, (Psalm 34:5). When Moses came out of the mount from communion with God, how illustrious was his face from that heavenly vision! Therefore, prayer for divine mercy and comfort sometimes exhibits itself in this language, "Cause thy face to shine" upon us; "and we shall be saved," (Psalm 80:3). On this wise the priests of old were to bless the children of Israel, "The Lord make his face shine upon thee, and be gracious unto thee." (Num. 6:25). These and other of the same expressions in scripture import that sometimes the Lord was pleased to give forth a shining glory from the oracle, and by this made known his presence to his people, and filled them with awful impressions of his majesty and mercy, (Exod. 40:34; Lev. 9:23; Num. 16:19, 42; 20:6; 1 Kings 8:11). This joyful light of God's countenance is like the sun rising on the face of the earth. It chases away the dark fears and discouragements of the night. Such heavenly joy shows the strength of faith in prayer, and the radiant appearances of God; yes, to this end all prayer should be directed, that our "joy may be full," (John 16:24).

4. A sweetness of affection to God, when the soul has gracious sentiments of God in prayer. Clouds of jealousies and suspicions of the divine mercy, as if God

were a hard master, are marvelously unbecoming a soul that should go to God as to a father; and here, from such unsuitable thoughts of infinite mercy, to hide the talent of prayer is greatly provoking. Where the apprehension of God's excellent goodness should work the heart into lovely thoughts of God. Man, but especially a saint, is *acervus beneficiorum Dei*, "an accumulated heap of divine favors;" and if nothing but the gifts of mercy should attract our hearts, yet in this we are every moment laden with his numerous benefits. But when the soul comes to perceive that all flows from the fountain of his eternal love, it makes prayer to be *res amorosa*, to be "filled with holy delights and joys." The ecstasies of love often rise on the soul in secret; and such divine affection, as Gerson said, it is *res ecstatica*, "it carries the soul beyond itself." Let the profane world say what they will, when spiritual ardors, like so many fragrant spices, flow out of the soul, "I love the Lord," David says, "because he hath heard my supplications," (Psalm 116:1). As answers of prayer flow from the love of the Father, (John 16:27), so suitable workings of holy affections flow from the hearts of children. When the soul is filled with gracious intimations, like those of the angelical voice to Daniel, "O Daniel, greatly beloved, O man of desires," to stand before the King of Saints, (Dan. 9:23; 10:11); or like that to the Holy Virgin, "Hail, thou that art highly favoured, the Lord is with thee," (Luke 1:28); how greatly does it inflame the heart to God!

5. Inward encouragements sometimes spring-in on the heart in prayer from remembrance of former experiments, which mightily animate the soul with fervency. When Moses calls to mind that God had forgiven and delivered, from Egypt until then, immediately follows a sweet intimation of mercy, "I have pardoned according to thy word," (Num. 14:19-20). When the soul considers the days of old, the years of ancient times, and "calls to remembrance" its former "songs in the night," he draws an argument out of the quiver of experience, "Will God be favourable no more? Can he forget to be gracious? Can he in anger shut up his tender mercies?" The soul concludes this thought to flow from its own "infirmity," (Psalm 77:5–10); for when God once hears a prayer, as coming from a child of his in covenant, prove our filial interest, we may sweetly rest assured in all things according to his will to be always heard.

6. A ready heart for thankfulness and service. The heart is brimful, and ready to flow-over in grateful memorials of his mercy. "What shall I render unto the Lord for all his benefits toward me?" (Psalm 116:12). As of old at temple-sacrifices there was music, so it ought to be now. While one is praying for mercy, the heart must be winding up and tuning for praise. The "vials full of the odors" of prayer are joined with harps for heavenly melody, (Rev. 5:8). When the "heart is fixed" or prepared, then follows song and praise, (Psalm 108:1). This streams from the sense of divine love; and love is the

fountain of thankfulness and of all sprightly and vigorous services. That prayer that does not end in cheerful obedience, is called by Cyprian *oratio sterilis and preces nudæ*, "barren and unfruitful, naked and without ornament;" and so we may glance upon the expression of holy James, the δεησις ενεργουμενη (James 5:16), "a working prayer" within will be working without, and demonstrate the labor of love.

OBSERVATION 2. The principal subject-matter of prayer, the mark, the white that the arrow of prayer is shot-at, the scope it aims at. There is usually some special sin unconquered, some untamed corruption, some defect, some pressing strait that drives the soul to prayer, and is the main burden of the spirit. Take notice how such a sin withers, or such a grace flourishes, or such a need is supplied on the opening of our hearts in prayer. "Watch unto prayer," (Eph. 6:18). Watch to perform it, and then to expound the voice of the divine oracle, and to know that ye are successful. Cry to thy soul by way of holy soliloquy, "Watchman, what of the night?" (Isa. 21:11).

OBSERVATION 3. Ensuing providences. Set a vigilant eye on succeeding passages; examine them as they pass before you; set a wakeful sentinel at the posts of wisdom. "That his name is near, his wondrous works declare," (Psalm 75:1); his name of truth, his glorious title of hearing prayers. When prayer is gone up by the help of the Spirit, mark how "all things work together for good," and note the connection there. The working of things together follows the intercession of the Spirit for all saints, (Rom. 8:27-28). God is pleased often to speak so clearly by his works, as if he said, "Here I am; I will 'guide thee continually. And thou shalt be like a watered garden, and like a spring of water, whose waters fail not,'" (Isa. 58:9, 11). Secret promises animate prayer, and open providences expound it. Cyrus was promised to come against Babylon for the church's sake. But Israel must ask it of God; and they had a word for it, that they should not seek his face in vain, (Isa. 45:4, 11, 19); and then follows Babylon's fall in the succeeding chapters. When we cry to the Lord in trouble, he sends his word of command, and heals us, (Psalm 107:19-20). There is a set time of mercy, a time of life. When Abraham had prayed for a son, the Lord told him, "At the time appointed I will return," (Gen. 15:2; 18:10, 14). In a great extremity, after the solemn fast of three days by the Jews in Shushan and the queen in her palace, on the fourth day at night the king could not sleep, and must hear the chronicles of Persia read; and then follows Haman's ruin, (Esther 4:16; 6:1). Prayer has a strange virtue to give quiet sleep sometimes to those like David, (Psalm 3:4-5), and sometimes a waking pillow for the good of the church. When Jacob had done wrestling, and the angel gone at the springing of the morning, then the good man saw the angel of God's presence in the face of Esau, (Gen. 33:1). Sometimes providence is not so quick. The martyrs' prayer, as to a complete answer from Christ, is deferred for a season; but long white robes are given to everyone, a triumphant frame of spirit, and they are told they should wait but a little season until divine justice should work-out the issue of prayer, (Rev. 6:11). The thunder on God's enemies comes out of the temple, the judgments roar out of Zion, the place of divine audience; but the means, and methods, and times of God's working are various, such as we little forethink, (Rev. 11:19; Joel 3:16). Submit all to his infinite wisdom; prescribe not, but observe, the embroidery of Providence; it is difficult to spell its characters sometimes, but it is rare employment. His works are searched into by such as delight in his providences, for all things are beautiful in his season, (Isa. 64:5; Psalm 111:2; Eccl. 3:11).

OBSERVATION 4. Mark your following communion with God. Inward answers make the soul vegete and lively; like plants, which, after the shining of the sun on rain, lift up their heads, and shoot-forth their flowers, (2 Sam. 23:4). A saint in favor does everything with delight. Answer of prayer is like oil to the spirits, and "beauty for ashes." The sackcloth of mournful fasting is turned to a wedding garment, (Isa. 61:3). He grows freer and yet humbly familiar with heaven. This is one I would wish you to pick acquaintance with, that can come and have what he will at court, (John 16:23). As the Lord once told a king by night, that Abraham was a prophet, and would pray for him, (Gen. 20:7). He was acquainted with the King of heaven. O blessed person! I hope there are many such among you, whose life is a continued prayer, as David that gave himself to prayer,

(Psalm 109:4). The Hebrew is literally, "But I prayer" which can be understood as "But I am in prayer always." He is all over prayer, prays at rising, prays at lying down, prays as he walks; he is always ready for prayer, like a prime favorite at court, that has the golden key to the privy stairs, and can wake his prince by night. Christians, there are such (whatever the besotted, profane world dreams) who are ready for spiritual ascents at all seasons, besides the frequency of set communions. His wings never weary. His willing spirit is flying continually, and makes God the "rock of his dwelling," לָבוֹא תָּדִיד in which he may upon all assaults have holy retirements, (Psalm 71:3).

Chapter 7:
Further Questions

But so much for the main question, with its branches. There are many particular queries of some weight that may attend the principal subject, and such I shall briefly reply to.

QUERY 1. "What is the proper time for secret prayer?"

ANSWER. Various providences, different temperaments and frames of spirits, motions from heaven, opportunities dictate variously. Some find it best at evening; others, in the night, when all is silent; others, at morning, when the spirits are freshest. I think, with respect to others, that conscientious prudence must guide in such cases, when others are retired, and the spirit in the best frame for communion.

QUERY 2. "How often should we pray in secret?"

ANSWER. If we consult scripture-precedent, we find David at prayer in the morning, (Psalm 5:3), our blessed Lord early before day in the morning, (Mark 1:35). Chrysostom advises, Νιψον ὧρο του σωματος την ψυχην, *etc.* "Wash thy soul before thy body;" for as the face and hands are cleansed by water, so is the soul by prayer. At another time our Lord went to secret prayer in the evening, (Matt. 14:23); and Isaac went to prayer in the eventide, (Gen. 24:63). David and Daniel prayed three times a day, (Psalm 55:17; Dan. 6:10); and once it is mentioned that David said, "Seven times a day do I praise thee," that is, very often, (Psalm 119:164). Such cases may happen that may require frequent accesses to the throne of grace in a day; but I humbly think, at the least once a day, which seems to be imported by that passage in our Lord's prayer, "Give us this day our daily bread;" since, after our Lord's appointment of secret prayer in the text, he gives this prayer as a pattern to his disciples.

QUERY 3. "When persons are under temptations or disturbance by passions, is it expedient then to pray?"

ANSWER. Since we are enjoined to "lift up holy hands, without wrath and doubting," (1 Tim. 2:8), I do not judge it so proper to run immediately to prayer; but with some foregoing ejaculations for pardon and strength against such exorbitances, and when in some measure cooled and composed, then speed to prayer, and take heed that the "sun go not down upon your wrath," (Eph. 4:26), without holy purgation by prayer. Though I must confess, a Christian should always endeavor to keep his course and heart in such a frame as not to be unfit for prayer on small warnings. The very consideration of our frequent communion with God should be a great bar to immoderate and exuberant passions.

QUERY 4. "Whether we may pray in secret, when others must necessarily take notice of us?"

ANSWER. I must confess, in certain homes, when a person can many times find no seasons but such as will fall under observation, I think he ought not to neglect secret duty, (if his heart is right before God), for fear of another noticing him. We must prevent it as much as may be, and especially watch our hearts against spiritual pride; and God may graciously turn it to a testimony and for example to others.

QUERY 5. "Whether we may be vocal in secret prayer, if we cannot so well raise or keep-up affection, or preserve the heart from wandering, without it?"

ANSWER. No doubt; but yet there must be used a great deal of wise caution about extending the voice. That of Tertullian, counselling persons at prayer, *Ne ipsis quidem manibus sublimiùs elatis, etc., ne vultu quidem in audaciam erecto. Sonos etiam vocis subjectos esse oportet; aut quantis arteriis opus est, si pro sono audiamur! etc. Qui clariùs adorant, proximis obstrepunt; imò prodendo orationes suas, quid minùs faciunt quam si in publico orent?* advises that both hands and countenance and voice should be ordered with great reverence and humility. "What arteries need we, if we think to be heard for noise! and what else do we by discovering our prayers, than if we prayed in public?" Yet surely if we can obtain some very private place, or when others are away from home, and the extension of the voice be found to some persons by long experience to be of use, such may lawfully improve it to their private benefit.

QUERY 6. "How to keep the heart from wandering thoughts in prayer?"

ANSWER. Although it is exceedingly difficult to attain so excellent a frame, yet by frequent reflecting on and remembering the eye of God in secret, by endeavoring to fix the heart with all possible watchfulness upon the main scope of prayer in hand, by being very sensible of our needs and indigence, by not studying of impertinent length, but rather being more frequent and short, considering God is in heaven and we on earth, and by exercise of holy communion, as we may through the implored assistance of the Spirit attain some sweetness and freedom, so likewise some more fixedness of spirit in our addresses before the Lord, (Eccl. 5:2).

QUERY 7. "What, if present answers seem not to correspond to our petitions?"

ANSWER. We must not conclude it by and by to be a token of displeasure, and say, with Job, "Show me wherefore thou contendest with me;" (Job 10:2); but acknowledge the sovereignty of divine wisdom and love in things that seem contrary to us in petitions for temporal mercies, and submit to the counsel of Elihu: "Since he giveth not account of any of his matters," neither can we find out the unsearchable methods of his holy ways to any perfection, (Job 33:13; 11:7).

There are other cases and scruples that might be treated of, as about prescript words in secret prayers, to which I need say but little; since such as are truly converted have the promise of the Spirit of God to assist and enable them, (Gal. 4:6; Rom. 8:26; Zech. 12:10; Acts

9:11), and they do not need to drink of another's bucket that have the fountain, nor use stilts and crutches that have spiritual strength; neither are words and phrases, but faith and holy groans, the nerves of prayer. Yet for some help to young beginners, doubtless it is of use to observe the style of the Spirit, as well as the heavenly matter of several prayers in the holy scriptures.

Neither do I need to press frequency to a holy heart that is fallen in love with spiritual communion; for he delights to be continually with him, the thoughts of God are so precious to him, (Psalm 23:6; 139:17-18). His soul is even sick of affection, and prays to be "stayed with" more of the "flagons," and "comforted with the apples" in greater abundance, (Song of Songs 2:5). To some (though I fear how few) ask how far it is lawful and expedient to withdraw for the necessity of the frail body in this vale of tears, it may be replied that "the Lord is very pitiful" and gracious to our frailties, that he had rather have mercy than sacrifice in some cases, (James 5:11; Hosea 6:6). Though I doubt these phoenixes are but rare that are in danger of expiring in prayer, as martyrs of divine love, as Gerson expresses.

Having now finished, with what brevity I could, the foregoing queries, I should treat about short, sudden, occasional prayers, commonly called "ejaculations;" but, indeed, that requires a set and just discourse. Yet, because of a promise above-recited, I shall give a few tastes of it, and then conclude with some application.

Chapter 8: Ejaculatory Prayer

Ejaculatory prayer is a sudden, short breathing of the soul towards heaven on instant and surprising emergencies. In holy persons it is quick and lively, rising from a vehement ardor of spirit, swifter than the flight of eagles, and keeps pace with a flash of lightning. It flies on the wings of a holy thought into the third heaven in the twinkling of an eye, and fetches auxiliary forces in times of straits.

There are many precedents recorded in sacred page upon great and notable occasions, with strange success. When good magistrates are busy in the work of reformation, let them imitate Nehemiah when redressing the profanation of the sabbath: "Remember me, O my God, concerning this," *etc.*, (Neh. 13:14, 22). When generals and captains go forth to war, observe Israel's appreciation to God, rather than acclamations to men, "The Lord thy God be with thee, as he was with Moses," (Joshua 1:17). In time of battles or pursuit of the enemy, valiant Joshua darts-up such a prayer as this, "O that the Lord would lengthen this triumphant day!" and the Lord heard his voice, (Joshua 10:12). The tribes beyond Jordan cried to the Lord in a battle with the Hagarites, (1 Chron. 5:20); Jehoshaphat, in a sore strait at Ramoth-Gilead, (2 Chron. 18:31); Samson, ready to perish at Lehi with thirst, and, when blind, exposed to contempt in the temple of Dagon, (Judges 15:18; 16:28); David, near stoning at Ziklag, and when flying from

Absalom in "the ascent of Mount Olivet," (1 Sam. 30:6; 2 Sam. 15:31); Elisha, at Dothan, compassed with a Syrian host, "Lord, open the young man's eyes," (2 Kings 6:17); in the midst of lawful and laborious callings, Boaz, to the reapers, "The Lord be with you," (Ruth 2:4; Psalm 129:8). We may pray "that our oxen may be strong to labour; that there is no breaking in, nor going out; that there is no complaining in our streets," (Psalm 144:14). It sanctifies the plough, as Jerome said of the fields of Bethlehem. *Quocunque te verteris, arator, stivam tenens, alleluja decantat, etc.*, "The tillers of the field, and the dressers of vineyards, sang David's psalms." It keeps the shop, and inclines the hearts of customers; it bars the doors, it quenches fire, it "blesseth thy children within thee," it "preserves thy going out and coming in," (Psalm 147:13; 121:8). Jacob found it to rest upon his children going a journey to Egypt, (Gen. 43:14). It closes the eyes with sweet sleep, it "gives songs in the night," and wakens the soul in the arms of mercy, (Job 35:10; Psalm 3:5; 4:8; 139:18). It sits at the helm when a storm rises at sea; it gives strength to anchors, and prosperous gales to the venturous merchant, (Psalm 107:28; Jonah 1:6). When, in the palace at dinner, Nehemiah presents the cup to his prince, he presents also a *michtam*, a "golden prayer" to the King of heaven, (Neh. 2:4). At the reading of the law Josiah was heard as to some secret cries to heaven, (2 Chron. 34:27). At a holy conference while on a journey the disciples occasionally pray, "Lord, increase our faith," (Luke 17:5). Jacob on his dying pillow, predicting future events to his children, falls into a holy rapture, "I have waited for thy salvation, O Lord," (Gen. 49:18). At sacred death in martyrdom Zechariah cries out, "The Lord look upon it, and require it," (2 Chron. 24:22); and Stephen, under a shower of stones, melts in prayers for the stony hearts that flung them, "Lord, lay not this sin to their charge," (Acts 7:60); and our blessed Savior in his greatest agonies makes a tender-hearted prayer. "Father, forgive them; for they know not what they do," (Luke 23:34). And, lastly, in the distresses of others, Eli puts-up a sudden petition for Hannah. "The God of Israel grant thee thy petition," (1 Sam. 1:17).

In these and many of the same cases, the holy word stores us with patterns for ejaculation in all extremities, which I cannot now digest and improve. Only in a few words let us take a view of the usefulness of such a sudden flight of the soul to heaven.

1. It helps us to a speedy preparative for all duties. With such an ejaculation, "let us lift our heart with our hands unto God in the heavens," (Lam. 3:41).

2. It is a guard against secret sins in the first risings, and the first assaults of temptation.

3. It does not suffer divine mercies to slip-by unobserved in a wakeful Christian, and proves a fruitful mother of gratitude and praise.

4. It sanctifies all our worldly employments, (1 Tim. 4:4-5); it fastens the stakes in the hedge of divine protection, and turns everything to a blessing.

5. It is a saint's buckler against sudden accidents, a present antidote against frights and evil tidings. It is good at all occasions, and consecrates to us, not only our meals, but every gasp of air, *etc.*

6. It is a sweet companion, that the severest enemies cannot abridge us of. Outward ordinances and closet duties they may cut off; the little "nail in the holy place" they may pluck out, (Ezra 9:8). But no labyrinth, no prison, not the worst of company can hinder this; *cælo restat iter*, in the very face of adversaries "we may lift our souls to God." No more of this. Let us briefly conclude with some uses.

Chapter 9: Uses

USE 1. To convince such of their dangerous state that neglect secret duties. That have no heart-communion, that draw no water out of this sealed fountain, (Song of Songs 4:12); but all they do is in public only. It is a suspicious token of hypocrisy, since the kernel and soul of religion lies so much in the heart and closet. Mark the phrase in the text, how it varies. "Thy Father which is in secret, which seeth in secret." God's eye is open on you in the closet; and if your eye is open on him, you may see a glorious beauty. The excellency of grace lies in making conscience of secret sins and secret duties.

USE 2. To examine such as perform secret duty, but they do not do it from a sincere principle. Like Amaziah, that prays, "but not with a perfect heart," (2 Chron. 25:2). Like Ahab, they mourn, but with crocodile tears. Such as do it only because they find precept or example for it, and, therefore, to quiet conscience, will in secret, but converse only in the shell and trunk of a duty; that rest in the naked performance, but does not matter whether they taste of the sweet streams that flow-in from heaven in the golden pipe of an ordinance; what account can such render, that go into their closets but, like Domitian, to catch only flies; and when the doors are shut to the world, their hearts are shut to heaven and communion with God? He that sees in secret beholds the evil frame of such a heart, and will one day openly punish it.

USE 3. To excite and awaken all to this excellent duty, and to manage it in an excellent manner. Would you live delightfully? Would you translate heaven to earth? Then keep-up communion in secret prayer, to know Him, to discern His face, to behold the luster of His eye that shines in secret. Remember the glorious Person that meets you in your closets. All the world does not yield such a glittering beauty as a gracious person sees, when he is in a happy frame at secret prayer. Shut your eyes when you come out; for all other objects are but vile and sordid, and not worth the glances of a noble soul. O! the sweetness, the hidden manna, that the soul tastes when in lively communion with God! Part of that which is "laid up for" saints in glory, let us relish a little our spirits with it, (Psalm 31:19).

1. Consider what amorous agonies the soul delights to conflict with in secret. Fears that raise confidence, humility that exalts, trembling's that embolden, bright clouds that shine upon our Israelites in the night, and darkness that enlightens, solitudes full of heavenly company, and tears brimful of joy, and holy sighs like a cooling wind in harvest, sweats of love, and sick fits that are symptoms of health, and holy fainting's that are the soul's cordials, a weariness to the flesh that is the healthful exercise of, and vigor to, the spirit, and a continual motion that never tires it. As Augustine said of divine love, *Illo feror quocunque feror; pondus meum,*

amor meus. "It is the weight of my soul; it carries me up and down in all that I speak, and all that I act."

2. Its ecstasies and heavenly raptures. These allure and draw the heart from earthly vanities; when the soul shuts its eyes to worldly delights, and says of laughter, with Solomon, "It is mad: and of mirth, What doeth it?" (Eccles. 2:2); cannot warm its thoughts at "the crackling of thorns under a pot," nor be joyful in the house of fools, (Eccles. 7:4, 6). It is the soul's pleasure to loathe pleasure itself; none so beautiful to him as Christ, "the chiefest among ten thousand;" (Song of Songs 5:10); no sweetness like that of the tree in the midst of the wood, "the tree of life in the midst of the Paradise of God;" he sits under it with great delight, while it drops sweeter than honey into his closet, (Song of Songs 2:3; Rev. 2:7; 1 Sam. 14:26).

3. Its admirable prophecies. Prayer stands on Mount Zion with a divining, presaging spirit: it foretells great things to the church's joy and its enemies' terror. Elijah at prayer in Horeb receives answer of the ruin of the house of Ahab, and is bid to go and "anoint Jehu the son of Nimshi king over Israel," (1 Kings 19:16). The two witnesses under the Romish defection "have power to smite the earth with plagues, as often as they will," (Rev. 11:6); consonant to what Tertullian said of old. *Votum Christianorum confusio nationum,* "The prayers of Christians confounded the nations." And so, it will shortly prove the doom of Babylon comes out of the temple. When the sanctuary is full of the smoke of the

incense of prayer, the seven angels come out with the seven last "vials full of the wrath of God," to pour them out upon the anti-christian world, (Rev. 15:7-8; 16:1). Prayer calculates and hastens the ruin of Rome. When the spirit of prayer is once poured out, it brings deliverance to mount Zion, and "gathers the nations into the valley of Jehoshaphat" to judgment, (Joel 2:21, 32; 3:1-2). Let us never be discouraged. If prayer works, and awakens Christ in the ship of the church, her storms will cease in a halcyon calm, (Luke 8:24).

4. It's comforting evidences. Secret prayer duly managed is a notable evidence of adoption. "Pray to thy Father who is, and sees, in secret," who "knows the secrets of thy heart," thy "groanings are not hid from" him, (Psalm 44:21; 38:9). None but a child of promise has this sweet freedom with God as a Father.

5. Its rewards and revenues. Nothing revives and cheers the spirit so much as answers of love and mercy from heaven. As it feasts the conscience with the royal dainties of sincerity, so it sets a luster on every mercy, as being the child of prayer. Our closets influence upon our shops, our ships, our fields, and all we enjoy, that they smell of divine blessing: as David said of precepts, (Psalm 119:56), the soul may say, "This I have, because I urged the promises."

USE 4. To pity the miserable blind world, that know not where true comfort, joy, and strength is to be found, (Gen. 27:28). That see no beauty in the ways of God, and feel no sweetness in communion with him;

that find no pleasure in closets, but play-houses, which Tertullian called "the devil's churches;" that cry out, with Esau, they "have enough," (Gen. 33:9). Alas! what "enough" can be in the creature, unless of dunghills, rattles, and vanities? O, how ignorant of heavenly treasures, of that fountain of mercies, whereof prayer drinks and refreshes the spirit of a saint! that know not that blessed "enough" of which Jacob speaks, that ocean of "all" things to be found in God! (Gen. 33:11). Now Europe is in flames, and the ark in danger, he does not care though the one is burnt, and the other in ashes, so long as he is safe. But if his concerns catch fire, he does not know to repair but to Endor or Ekron, (1 Sam. 28:7; 2 Kings 1:2). Such have no acquaintance with, no help from, God, no interest in the keeper of souls. The world is a deplorable hospital, the great lazar-house of sick, lame, and impotent persons, as Gerson describes it, that have no face nor heart to go to the Physician of souls.

But ah! most lamentable is the state of some prostitute wretches of our age, that are, I fear, almost incurably gone with spiritual ulcers in their lungs, and eating, putrid cancers in their tongues; that breathe nothing but venom, and openly spit-out their rotten atheistical jeers against the spirit of prayer, and make a mock at communion with God; that scoff at what God has promised as one of the choicest tokens of his love to the church, and symptoms of the glory of the latter times, (Zech. 12:10; Joel 2:28, 32; Rom. 10:13; John 7:39), when God will turn such Ishmaels into the desert, and their drunken songs shall expire in dreadful howling's; (Amos 8:10; Job 30:31); profaner than many heathens, that in the primitive times had some reverence for Christian worship, though they persecuted. But those of this adulterous Romish age, like brute beasts, speak evil of what they are ignorant of, and are in danger to "perish utterly in their own corruption," (2 Peter 2:12). Pity such, if there is yet hope, and commend their condition to God's mercy, and penitent sorrow; that they may weep here, where tears prick; not in hell, where they scald and burn, and swell that river of brimstone.

In the meantime, O! ye that fear the Lord, be diligent to observe and interpret messages after secret prayer; for the life and joy of a Christian is improved by it. God has declared himself graciously pleased with secret prayer, so as to send an angel, that glorious creature, to fly into Daniel's chamber, and he "weary with flying," he moved so swiftly, מֻעָף בִּיעָף *volans in lassitudine*, as the original text expresses it, (Dan. 9:21). What a high expression is this, that even angels are represented weary with hasty flights to bring saints their answers! and of what great account does the Lord esteem his praying people, that angels are expressed to be tired in bringing tidings of mercy!

USE 5. Meditate on the glory of heaven, where all our prayers shall be turned into praises. When every sigh below shall be an accent to the heavenly music above, and the fears of the valley shall be turned into orient gems in the diadem of glory. Here we groan under needs and desires, empty within, and live on the craving hand; but there we have palms in the hand, white robes, and everlasting joys on the heads and hearts of saints.

FINIS

Other Helpful Books on Prayer by Puritan Publications

Gospel Worship, or, The Right Manner of Sanctifying the name of God in General, in Hearing the Word, Receiving the Lord's Supper, and Prayer by Jeremiah Burroughs (1599-1646)

The Spirit of Prayer by Nathaniel Vincent (1639-1697)

Sermons, Prayers, and Pulpit Addresses by Alexander Henderson (1583-1646)

The Christian's Duty and Safety in Evil Times by Christopher Love (1618-1651)

The Christian's Combat Against the Devil by Christopher Love (1618-1651)

How to Serve God in Private and Public Worship by John Jackson (1600-1648)

The Reformed Apprentice Volume 4: A Workbook on Private Devotions by C. Matthew McMahon

The Armor of God by Paul Bayne (1573-1617)

www.ingramcontent.com/pod-product-compliance
Lightning Source LLC
LaVergne TN
LVHW041549070426
835507LV00011B/996